BABYLON

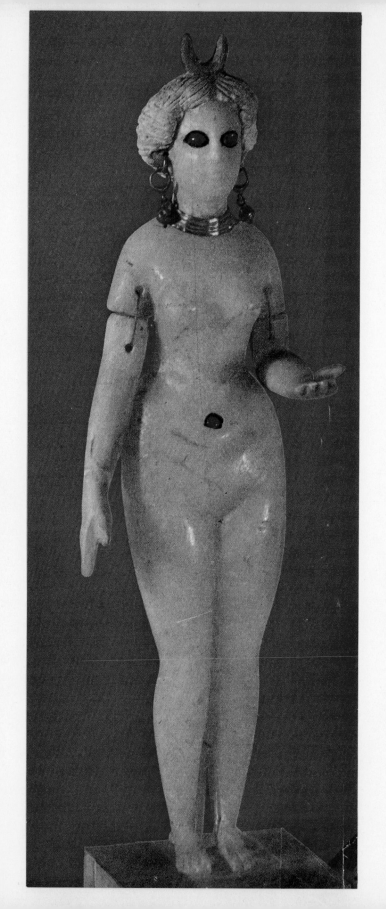

BABYLON

9

ALBERT CHAMPDOR

Translated from the French and adapted by
ELSA COULT

LONDON   ELEK BOOKS
NEW YORK   G. P. PUTNAM'S SONS

Published in Great Britain by
ELEK BOOKS LIMITED
14 Great James Street
London, W.C.1

Published in the United States of America by
G. P. PUTNAM'S SONS
210 Madison Avenue
New York City 16
New York

Published in Canada by
THE RYERSON PRESS
299 Queen Street West
Toronto 2B

Printed in Great Britain
by W. & J. Mackay & Co Ltd, Chatham

CONTENTS

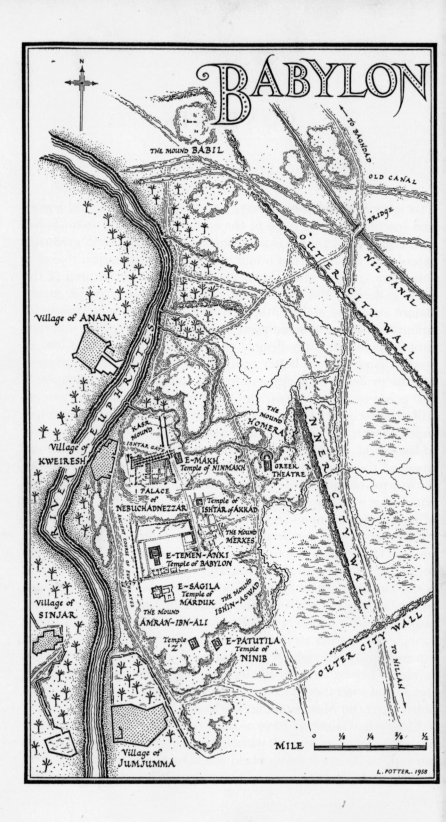

BABYLON

N

To BAGHDAD

THE MOUND BÁBIL

OLD CANAL

BRIDGE

O U T E R   C I T Y   W A L L

NIL CANAL

Village of ANANA

THE MOUND HOMERA

R I V E R   E U P H R A T E S

Village of KWEIRESH

KASR MOUND ISHTAR GATE

E-MÁKH Temple of NINMÁKH

GREEK THEATRE

I N N E R   C I T Y   W A L L

PALACE of NEBUCHADNEZZAR

Temple of ISHTAR of ÁKKAD

THE MOUND MERKES

ANCIENT COURSE OF EUPHRATES

E-TEMEN-ÁNKI Temple of BABYLON

Village of SINJAR

E-SÁGILA Temple of MÁRDUK

THE MOUND ISHIN-ASWAD

THE MOUND ÁMRAN-IBN-ÁLI

Temple 'Z'

E-PÁTUTILA Temple of NINIB

OUTER CITY WALL

TO HILLAH

Village of JUMJUMMÁ

MILE   0   ⅛   ¼   ⅜   ½

L. POTTER. 1958

FOREWORD

THE story of Babylon has always been a subject of colourful legend and speculation since some of the earliest writings of man. It has now begun to take shape as an authentic historical record, gradually pieced together in the last hundred years of archaeological research. But there are still many gaps. We know virtually nothing of the early history of the city, except that there was a temple there. Before about the eighteenth century B.C. Babylon was apparently unimportant; yet at some point during that century she emerged into the limelight fully-fledged and competent to take the lead in world affairs. We are better equipped to follow her later fortunes, but the evidence is patchy and in part controversial. Excavation is still going on all over Iraq, and there are thousands of documents still to be deciphered. The sheer quantity of the material unearthed, much of which is dispersed in museum collections in various parts of the world, presents a formidable problem to the historian, and many of the vital dates of the period are still in dispute. Yet the discoveries already made have revolutionized historical thinking within our own time, and there has emerged a remarkable picture, of human achievement in this distinguished region of the world.

Babylon's swift rise from obscurity to fame was not in itself unique. Other cities before her had been known to achieve sudden supremacy in Mesopotamian history. What is much more striking is the fact that she retained an influential position in the ancient world far longer than any other capital in her time. Vicissitudes came, one after another; the city was twice sacked, and fell under foreign domination for long periods; raids and invasions went on intermittently throughout her history. But twelve centuries were to elapse before Babylon finally had to give up her independent status, and even then it took another 200 years before her influence faded from the Mesopotamian world.

Clearly it was not by force of arms that Babylon maintained her distinctive position, though without some degree of military success her reputation in a warring world would have been seriously undermined and her wealth reduced to nothing. It was the impact of her culture upon Western Asia that won respect. Babylonian literature, art, religion, law and scientific enterprise together expressed a remarkable harmony of purpose. From the very first the Babylonians had shown that they were already a highly developed civilized community with strong traditions of thought and behaviour, inspired and sustained by their religious belief. Their great god was the Creator of the Universe, who had commanded that order and equity should prevail. It was the lot of man to obey. And in seeking to establish order and equity the Babylonians were both business-like and practical. Technical ingenuity, enterprise, and commonsense produced results. A vigorous trading policy attracted interest abroad, and soon the Babylonian script and tongue were used extensively in diplomatic as well as commercial correspondence. The necessary linguistic proficiency would presumably have had to be attained with the help of the religious literature, which was a rich source of Babylonian teaching. Law, medicine, economy, ethics, poetry and mathematics, mythology and magic as recorded by the priests and scholars of Babylon were thus available for all who studied her language and could spread her wisdom far afield.

Who were the Babylonians and how did their ideas and traditions originate? What were the operative factors in their success? To be able to answer these questions with any degree of certainty we should need to know a lot more than we do. But modern research has shown that Babylonian culture flowered relatively late in Mesopotamian history. The civilization of Sumer, with which it had close affinities, was flourishing more than a thousand years earlier. Predecessors of the Sumerians are to be found in upland settlements of unknown antiquity. And the advent of man in and around this region is distinguished not only by remoteness in time but by a remarkable quality of achievement which shows itself from the first at a number of sites. The people who settled near the Tigris and Euphrates seem always to have been richly endowed with creative gifts.

One of the most interesting developments attributed to Mesopotamia is that of the art of writing. This, by the beginning of the third millennium B.C., was firmly established in Sumer, whose documents mark the beginning of historical times. When or where it was first introduced as a systematic means of conveying a message we do not know; but it is reasonable to suppose that it developed in response to a fairly urgent need. Markings of various kinds on pottery and on bone implements are attested from ancient times;

the need to indicate ownership must have arisen very early, and as soon as goods began to be exchanged some system of labelling or even numbering them would have had to be devised. But the actual recording of transactions, such as we find on some of the earliest clay tablets, seems to have been a comparatively late idea. The process itself was simple enough with the aid of a reed and a piece of damp clay that retained its markings when dried in the sun. But such a procedure implies other things; in learning not only to value property, but to evaluate it in terms of the other goods he had come to require, man had found it necessary to formulate a business-like system to achieve his ends. And one good reason for doing so may have been that he was some distance away from the various sources of vital material.

On the fringe of Mesopotamia other major innovations had long since been established. Civilized communities at least as early as the fifth millennium B.C. had been growing up in northern Iraq, Anatolia, and to the west on the plateaux of Iran. They had mastered the art of metallurgy and introduced the potter's wheel; they had solved the problem of transport by the use of pack animals, draught oxen, wheeled vehicles, and sailing craft. Some of their pottery is amongst the finest ever made, as for instance the painted ware from Tell Halaf on the Habur, north of the Euphrates. Amulets and seals were already in use, and shrines and houses were built of moulded bricks, dried in the sun, or in some cases of stone. The origin of some of these settlements is difficult to determine, but it is apparent that for some thousands of years before historical times the hill-country, steppes and plateaux of this region offered a strong inducement to man as a living environment. And the evidence suggests that although commercial interchange was not entirely lacking, these communities were relatively self-contained and essential commodities easily accessible. In such circumstances there was no particular incentive to keep detailed records, nor was there suitable material at hand for doing so.

Had the people of these earlier communities been able to write, at least in a form which we could now read, they might well be accredited with much of the distinction which now goes to Sumer, for their accomplishments were also considerable and bear the marks of original genius. The lengthy period of settlement which preceded the emergence of the Sumerians is perhaps best considered in a geographical context, since Mesopotamia is a country which has undergone considerable changes in the course of time.

Both the climate and the land itself must always have made life

difficult and uncertain for human inhabitants, a never-ending tax
on human ingenuity. In prehistoric times the sea extended inland
some distance north of Baghdad, nearly 400 miles from the present
shore-line, and the two rivers, separated by a great tract of desert,
flowed into the sea some 60 miles apart. Both rivers rise in the high
Armenian range, plunging steeply down over a considerable distance in northern Iraq, and depositing large quantities of silt in the
estuarine plains. This process over the centuries led to the formation
of a vast tract of delta as the waters of the Tigris and Euphrates
gradually merged, and the sea-margin was continually pushed
back before the accumulation of alluvial deposits. When the earliest
Sumerian city-states grew up on this delta in the fourth millennium
B.C., Ur and Lagash were close to the swamps and marshland that
fringed the coast, still some 160 miles inland from the modern
shore-line. The marshes always played an important part in Mesopotamian life; they are frequently alluded to in the literature and
are featured in the later reliefs of Sennacherib of Assyria in his
famous 'War in the Marshes'.

On the alluvial plains of southern Iraq the soil is potentially
fertile like that of the Nile Valley; but it requires far more attention. The ancient Egyptians had few agricultural problems; their
sunny valley was richly fertilized and watered by the regular
inundations of the Nile, and irrigation was a relatively simple business. In Mesopotamia man had to battle constantly with the
elements. The dwellers on the southern plains could never count
on nature. Their rainfall was uncertain and often negligible, and
the rivers on which they had to depend for their water-supply were
liable to sudden and unpredictable flooding. In spring and early
summer, with the melting of the Armenian snows, considerable
havoc amongst crops and stock could be caused by the tremendous
force of water that swept down from the north. Down in the plains
the summer months, lasting well into November, were stifling, and
the sun burnt up the land and produce; often it became necessary
to hand-feed the flocks from carefully-rationed stores. Nevertheless
the early settlers of Sumer learnt by ingenuity and great diligence
to harness the water and make the most of their land. Their
irrigation system, neat, complex, and rigorously maintained, won
them a prosperity hitherto unattained.

Farther up the valleys, in the steppes and in the hill-country to
the north, there was recurrent disruption from heavy rains. Wide-
spread flooding has been a characteristic of the Tigris-Euphrates
region at all periods, and to judge by the many allusions to be found

in the ancient texts, they obviously presented a considerable problem in administration. In the Mari district, for instance, a governor of the nineteenth century B.C. reported to his master that the Habur, a tributary of the Euphrates, had burst its banks and 300 acres of land were under water; torrential rain had delayed the sheep-shearing, which would now take twice as long as there were still a hundred sheep to be shorn. In the famous Code of Hammurabi of Babylon, at about the same period, we find perhaps the earliest recognition in law of an 'Act of God': 'If a debt is outstanding against a seignior and Adad (God of Rain) has inundated his field or a flood has ravaged it, or through lack of water grain has not been produced in the field, he shall not make any return of grain to his creditor in that year; he shall cancel his contract-tablet and he shall pay no interest for that year.' Assurbanipal, who reigned in Assyria during the seventh century B.C., referred more than once to unusually heavy rainfall: 'At that time the wall inside the city of Nineveh . . . whose foundation had given way and its turret fallen, on account of the abundant showers and heavy rain which Adad had yearly sent upon my land during my reign, . . . had become old and its walls weak. . . .' And again, this time with obvious concern: 'Since I took my seat upon the throne of the father who begat me, Adad has sent his rains, Ea (God of Water) has opened up his fountains, the forests have been thriving exceedingly, the reeds of the marshes have shot up so high there is no getting through them. The young of the lions grew up therein in countless numbers . . . they became fierce and terrible, through their devouring of herds, flocks and people. With their roaring the hills resound, the beasts of the field are terrified. They keep bringing down the cattle of the plain, they (keep) shedding the blood of men. The shepherds and herdsmen weep at the lions'. . . . The villages are in mourning day and night. Of the deeds of these lions they told me. In the course of my march into . . . their lairs I broke up. . . .' This inscription accounts perhaps for the royal sport of lion-hunting, practised with evident success by Assurbanipal and depicted in his famous 'Lion Frieze' now in the British Museum. That the havoc caused by flooding was only too familiar to the Assyrians is evident from the many inscriptions of these warrior kings describing their laying waste of cities 'like a flood'.

The same problem exists in modern Iraq. A recent report referred to an exceptionally heavy rainfall with the Tigris in spate to the extent that Baghdad was threatened with one of the worst floods in its history. Communications in the north were severed, but new flood control and irrigation measures appear to have been effective. There have been many occasions in the past when human effort was of no avail, defences crumbled, and large sections of the population were swept away.

It is therefore hardly surprising that, as Seton Lloyd points out in discussing the early Sumerian documents: 'One fact that all the chroniclers . . . seem fairly agreed upon is that the first really important landmark in history was a great flood.' This, according to the early scribes, caused a long gap in the royal succession; after the first group of kings, 'then came the Flood, and after the Flood kingship again descended from on high.' Archaeological excavation has in fact produced evidence of a flood at four of the early Sumerian sites, but the stratification showed that they belonged to different periods. On a tablet in Sumerian from Nippur is recorded a story of the Deluge closely akin to that of the Bible, and another, very similar, is contained in the Epic of Gilgamesh from the Akkadian texts of Assurbanipal's library at Nineveh. In the latter, which is better preserved, a patriarch whose home is at Shuruppak on the Euphrates, Utu-napishtim by name, is warned by the god Ea:

'Tear down this house, build a ship! . . .
. . . Aboard the ship take thou the seed of all living things
The ship that thou shalt build
Her dimensions shall be to measure.
Equal shall be her width and her length. . . .'

And Utu-Napishtim, not without difficulty, built and launched his ship, laden with his family and kin, all living beings, silver and gold; and he battened it down.

'I watched the appearance of the weather
The weather was awesome to behold. . . .
. . . Consternation over Adad reaches to the heavens,
Turning to blackness all that had been light
The (wide) land was shattered like (a pot)!
For one day the south storm (blew)
Gathering speed as it blew (submerging the mountains)
Overtaking the people like a battle.
No one can see his fellow,
Nor can the people be recognized from heaven.
. . . Six days and (six) nights
Blows the flood wind, as the south storm sweeps the land
When the seventh day arrived . . .

. . . The sea grew quiet, the tempest was still, the flood ceased.
I looked at the weather; stillness had set in.
. . . And all of mankind had returned to clay.
The landscape was as level as a flat roof.
I opened a hatch, and light fell on my face.
Bowing low, I sat and wept,
Tears running down my face . . .
. . . On Mount Nisir the ship came to a halt.
Mount Nisir held the ship fast,
Allowing no motion . . .
. . . I sent forth and set free a dove.
The dove went forth, but came back;
There was no resting-place for it and she turned round.
. . . Then I sent forth and set free a raven.
The raven went forth and, seeing that the waters had dimin-
ished,
He eats, circles, caws, and turns not round.
Then I let out (all) to the four winds
And offered a sacrifice. . . .'

From early times, therefore, it seems that the Mesopotamians
were brought up on the story of the Flood much as it was later to
be recorded in the Hebrew Chronicles. Presumably one of the
prehistoric floods, possibly a major transgression of the sea, was
more devastating than the rest, carrying away almost a total
population. All people and events belonging to pre-Deluge times,
including kings, gods, and heroes, thus became assigned by the
later chroniclers to a vague mythology spanning an indefinite
period of time. But whatever their literature told them of the havoc
wrought in a remote past, the inhabitants of the river banks could
have needed no reminding of what was still a perennial danger
requiring incessant vigilance.

In terms of climate and physical features, the Tigris-Euphrates
region in Iraq thus comprises two distinctive environments, north
and south, the lands which came to be known respectively as
Assyria and Babylonia. Neither was particularly congenial; but
both had excellent potentialities for livelihood. The rugged land of
the north, with its bitter winters, drenching rains, and violent
summer storms, was nevertheless close to the rich mineral resources
of Anatolia, including abundant gold, silver, copper, lead and iron.
Timber from the foothills was plentiful, and limestone easily
obtainable, if not always of good quality. There was, as we have

seen, no shortage of water; cereals, fruit-trees and vines might be damaged by bad weather, but they grew easily and profusely along the slopes of the foothills. Pasture was good and large herds and flocks could be maintained. In the torrid plains of the south, on the other hand, man's wits were his greatest asset. Timber was lacking here, and so was stone; the date palm grew, and reeds in abundance, but the raising of cereals required strict maintenance of canals. Naphtha and bitumen, the latter an especially valued resource of this region, were available from the sub-soil; but the prime material on which the settler had to depend for shelter and storage of grain was mud and clay, dried into bricks or fired into pottery shapes that were handy for every conceivable domestic purpose.

As the sea gradually retreated, leaving a vast expanse of rich alluvium and treacherous marsh, small groups of settlers began to venture down from the hills and plateaux to the north. These people, who appear to have come first from Iran, then from Anatolia, and later again from Iran, were skilled craftsmen and architects, each successive community improving and adapting their techniques. At Uruk for instance, the Biblical Erech, impressive monuments had already begun to appear. There were palaces and temples, and a shrine built on a raised platform, the forerunner of the *ziggurat* which became a central feature of Sumerian and Babylonian building. Careful planning went into this early architecture; it was neat, symmetrical, and colourfully decorated in mosaic form by means of brightly painted clay cones arranged in patterns. At 'Uqair there were wall-paintings arranged in a series of registers, with a band of plain colour at the bottom, followed by bright geometric patterns, and above these processions of figures, some human and some possibly mythical beasts. Two animal figures, thought to be lions or leopards, guarded the altar; and there were also a number of figures carved on stone in relief. These builders and sculptors were of Anatolian origin, with a distinctive pottery quite unlike that of their predecessors. Crude picture signs on clay tablets had now appeared, and with the advent of a fresh wave of immigrants towards the end of the fourth millennium B.C. we find a noticeable advance in the systematization of writing. This last phase before the Sumerian period proper, which is largely distinguished by the appearance of official king-lists, produced carvings of great beauty, both in relief and in the round, and amongst them was a life-sized head in marble. Stone was non-existent in the delta. Extensive trading had clearly begun.

The plains and marshes could not have held out much promise of

an easier life; but perhaps the greatest inducement to settle, apart
from an abundance of fish and fowl, had been the ever-reliable
date-palm, year in and year out yielding its nutritious crop and
valuable by-products: fruit, a staple food; date wine, kernels,
matting, basketry, roofing, stems for columns, fibre for rope. And
once the barley yield was eighty-six times the sowing, as recorded in
texts of the third millennium B.C., the settlers were well able to
produce far more than they required for their own needs. Dates and
barley—the chief exports still of Iraq. For trade was of the utmost
importance to the people of the plains. Good quality stone was
highly prized, timber was useful and metal indispensable. Wool,
perhaps cotton, and raw hide were needed, as well as luxuries in the
form of lapis-lazuli and other precious stones, shells, and fine fruits
and wines.

To what extent the Sumerians were a distinctive race of people
who superseded or absorbed the earlier communities in the delta
region, we do not know. Eridu, according to tradition, was the
oldest city of Sumer, and excavations there have revealed a long
series of temples dating from the time of the first settlers in the
area. These temples were built on the same lines as those of the
historical period of Sumer, and appear to have been dedicated to
one of the principal gods of Sumerian religion. The name of this
god was Enki, later called Ea by the Semites. He was lord of the
earth, and god of the sweet waters that surround the earth, and
also god of wisdom and magic; sometimes he was called Lord of the
Abyss. Legend has it that he built at Eridu a sea-house of silver and
lapis lazuli like sparkling light. Religion, the central feature of
Sumerian life, was deeply rooted in prehistoric beliefs.

The Sumerian pantheon was highly complex. To interpret its
meaning at all adequately it will be necessary to await the trans-
lation of a large body of literature, only a small part of which has
so far been published. But enough perhaps is known to distinguish a
coherent religious system, with two prevailing themes which are
closely interlinked: the establishment of order out of chaos, by the
various great gods of the elements; and the cycle of death and resurrection, associated with the age-old conception of the mother-
goddess and the god of fertility. Amid a host of other deities the
sun, moon and planet Venus are also represented, the last of these,
who became the Semitic goddess Ishtar, being also Goddess of Love
and War. There was also a great variety of demons and evil spirits
to whose machinations sickness and ill-fortune were ascribed and
who had to be driven away by magic and incantation.

One of the Sumerian myths speaks of the Mountain of Heaven and Earth. It would seem that *an-ki*, heaven and earth united, in other words the universe, was conceived as a mountain whose peak was the top of heaven and whose bottom was the earth. At Babylon the great *ziggurat* of unknown date was known as E-temen-anki, the House of the Foundation of Heaven and Earth. The organization of the earth, according to the Sumerians, was chiefly the work of Enlil and Enki. Enlil, whose name we meet in Babylonian literature, was a god of the atmosphere; his father, An, carried off heaven and Enlil took charge of the earth, causing 'the good day to come forth'. . . . He 'brought forth seed from the earth and established abundance in the land'. It was he who chose kings on earth and conferred on them authority over mankind. An inscription of Lugal-zaggisi, an ancient king of Erech, runs as follows: 'When Enlil, king of the land, had delivered the kingship of the land to Lugal-zaggisi, had made him to prosper, and had caused the land to submit to his power. . . .' In the time of Hammurabi, of the First Dynasty of Babylon, the functions of Enlil were delegated to Marduk, god of Babylon, but the Prologue to his Code of Laws is full of allusions to Sumerian deities: 'When . . . Enlil, lord of heaven and earth, the determiner of the destinies of the land, determined for Marduk, the first-born of Enki, the Enlil functions over all mankind. . . . At that time Anum (An) and Enlil named me to promote the welfare of the people.' Marduk, then, was regarded as the son of the Sumerian Enki, who when earth and heaven were separated ruled over the waters. Marduk took over the rôle of Enlil, lord of the earth. It was not legend, but fact, that earth had appeared out of the waters in the region of Sumer and Babylon. Marduk, therefore, was the Creator God; and because the earth which he had formed was rich, the vegetation it produced was his, to give or withhold according to the extent to which men obeyed his commands. He therefore also took over the rôle of a fertility god, and it was from him that the kings, his earthly representatives, derived their sovereignty.

This idea is fundamental to Sumerian beliefs. Sumer consisted of a handful of city-states, each with its own deity. Kingship was not hereditary. Each god had a human steward or king to manage his estate; but the god remained the real ruler and nothing could be done until his advice by means of omens had been ascertained. Each city had temples or shrines devoted to the worship of a number of gods in addition to that dedicated to its own particular deity. In the course of time, different cities achieved supremacy

[1] Primitive Mesopotamian art: Clay figurine.

[2] Mari: Detail from plaque, shell inlaid; third millennium B.C. (*Louvre*.)

[3] Prehistoric Mesopotamian figurine with serpent. (*Louvre.*)

[4] Sumerian plaque; third millennium B.C. (*Louvre.*)

[5] Sumerian statue from al 'Ubaid: Kur-lil, a priestly official. (*British Museum.*)

[6] Head of a lion from al 'Ubaid. (*British Museum.*)

[7]

[8]

[7] Terracotta figurine from Mesopotamia. (*Louvre.*)

[8] Sumerian figure from a temple at Mari. Third millennium B.C. (*Louvre.*)

Joh: The Sumerian ruler of Lagash, Urnanshe, with his son; third millennium B.C. (*Louvre*.)

[10] Urnanshe, ruler of Lagash, with his family: plaque to commemorate the building of a temple.

In the top left-hand corner Urnanshe carries a basket of mud to mould the first brick; at the bottom on the right he is seen celebrating the completion of the work. Third millennium B.C. (*Louvre.*)

[11] Telloh: Stone plaque of the High Priest Dudu of Lagash; third millennium B.C. (*Louvre.*)

[12] Libation Vase of Gudea, ruler of Lagash. The vase is dedicated to Ningizidda, who represented natural vitality. End of third millennium B.C. (*Louvre*.)

[13] Detail from the base of the statue of Ur-Ningirsu, son of Gudea. End of third millennium B.C. (*Louvre*.)

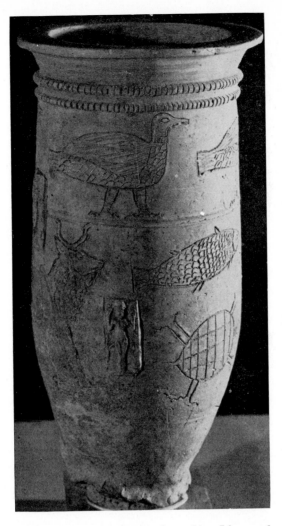

[14] Larsa: Vase depicting the goddess Ishtar and
various sacred emblems. Terracotta. End of third
millennium B.C. (*Louvre.*)

[15] Woman holding aryballos; late third or early second millennium B.C. (*Louvre*.)

[16] The famous stele commemorating the victory of Naram-Sin, King of Akkad and the 'Four Regions'. Late third millennium B.C. (*Louvre*.)

[17] King-list from Larsa, in terracotta,
inscribed on all four sides; early second
millennium B.C. (*Louvre.*)

[18] Telloh: an expressive portrait of a Mesopotamian deity, in terracotta. (*Louvre.*)

[19] Copper figure from Mesopotamia: early second millennium B.C. (*Louvre.*)

[20] Babylonian figure of a musician in terracotta. (*Louvre.*)

[21] Babylonian harp-player in terracotta. (*Louvre.*)

[22] Pazuzu, demon of the winds. These small figures were used by the Babylonians as a charm hung round the neck, to protect them from sickness and fever. (*Louvre.*)

[23] Top of a stele from the First Dynasty of Babylon, thought to represent Hammurabi, King of Babylon. (*British Museum.*)

over the others, but this seems not to have affected the status of the gods; for instance one of the most important of the Sumerian gods was at all times Enlil, but so far as we know his city, Nippur, never at any time had any political importance.)

The gods were imagined in human form and endowed with human emotions and desires. The temple was therefore quite literally the house of the god where he dwelt in the person of his statue, and had to be clothed and fed. Temple organization neces-sarily played a vital part in the economic and social life of the com-munity. Each temple, and there might be several in a city, owned land, and was a great centre of business. At this period also, the priests were largely responsible for the administration of justice; cases were heard at the temple gates, and when parties to a dispute had to swear oaths in the name of the god, this was done in the temple. Each temple maintained a large staff, some of whom were slaves. They either received daily allowances or had to give a fixed proportion of their produce to the temple, and were liable for military service. In return for their services the temple undertook their upkeep all the year round, supplying them with seed corn, agricultural implements and plough cattle.

The principal crop was barley, which was delivered to the temple. Some of the grain was used for cattle fodder, some went to the temple brewery, but most of it was ground into flour.) Fresh-water fish were also regularly supplied to the temple, and oxen were kept both for the plough and for meat. The god had regular meals morning and evening, and extra-special ones on feast days. In practice this meant that the food was placed on the altar and the deity feasted on the savoury smells. The sacred diet was varied—mutton, fish, bread, flour, cakes, butter, fruit, honey and beer—and everything had to be of the highest quality. The minor deities who formed the divine household had also to be catered for. Undoubtedly the supplies of food offered to the god were taken as perquisites by the priests, and in later periods the buying and sell-ing of such perquisites was common. Priests and temple staff, bakers, brewers, weavers and so on also had to be supported. In only a small temple the total number of servants and dependants was about 1,200.

It is clear from both textual and archaeological evidence that the Early Dynastic city-states of Sumer enjoyed great prosperity. Their principal source of wealth was agriculture, but other industries flourished too, such as cloth-making, metal-working, carpentry and many other crafts. This meant importing many raw materials.

Cargoes of timber from abroad are mentioned in royal inscriptions, but the chief evidence for foreign trade comes from excavations, particularly the so-called Royal Cemetery at Ur. This produced an astonishingly rich collection including furniture, jewellery, vessels of gold, silver and bronze, gold and bronze weapons, and musical instruments. The most probable source of copper is Oman or possibly Sinai, because at both these places the local ore has a slight admixture of nickel which analysis has shown to be present in the copper objects from Sumer. Much of the gold was alluvial, possibly from the gold-bearing rivers of Armenia, Nubia and Cilicia, and silver may have come from Asia Minor. Lapis-lazuli, which was believed by the Sumerians to have magical properties, and which they used in great quantities, may have been brought from Afghanistan, the nearest known source. Another semi-precious stone much favoured by Sumerian jewellers was carnelian, which occurs both in Persia and north-west India. That there was indeed trade in carnelian with India is indicated by the presence at Ur of beads of carnelian with bleached patterns. This peculiar technique is also attested at the Indian site of Harappa, in levels contemporary with the later Agade period in Mesopotamia. There is a strong probability that the beads found at Ur were of Indian manufacture; other imports from this same area were seals bearing designs and writing which can be paralleled at Harappa.

All this evidence for foreign trade therefore indicates that during the early part of the third millennium B.C., if not somewhat earlier, there was traffic from Syria and Asia Minor down the great rivers to the Persian Gulf and over the mountains to Persia and Baluchistan. The wonderful display of the Royal Tombs, which may have been associated with a religious rite, shows that the cities of Sumer had sufficient wealth to acquire foreign commodities in considerable quantities.

It is accordingly not surprising that writing should have developed in these circumstances. The Early Dynastic people of Sumer, like their immediate predecessors, who are sometimes also regarded as Sumerians, were methodical people. The neatness and intelligent planning of their buildings and their fondness for symmetrical patterns are evidence enough of the orderliness which they admired. They were also mathematically-minded, devising a system of numeration that was partly sexagesimal and partly decimal. Their tables of weights were based on what could be carried by a man or an animal, but they also used fractions. The day was divided into twelve 'double hours', and the circle into 360 parts. Geometry, algebra, and astronomy were extensively employed in calculations required for religious purposes, and in the practical field of agricultural development. They served their gods; the temples had to be maintained at the highest possible level. Precious commodities had to be brought from far afield in exchange, weight by weight, or according to an official scale of charges, for what they could produce from the soil. It was necessary to account for every detail of a transaction, and to be able to draw up contracts which could bear the official seal of the ruler and other witnesses. Agents had to be entrusted with temple orders for goods, and long-distance travelling was far from safe. Meticulous records helped to prevent disputes. And although most trading was carried on in the name of the palace or temple, the occasional margin of profit enabled private individuals to amass small personal fortunes, which had to be noted on separately-kept accounts. But it must be remembered that although in the natural course of things writing was extended to the sphere of religious literature and royal records, it is not possible on the present evidence to infer how much of this related to Sumerian doctrine and nothing else. The development of writing itself appears to have been their innovation, and it was one of a very high order; but what they wrote about may have related to ideas and beliefs that were very much older. The gods they named in their writings may have been gods of an earlier race, adapted, as the Babylonians later adapted theirs, and the Hittites, Assyrians, and even the Greeks after them, to conform with their own particular way of life. The Sumerian mythology is clearly very ancient in conception, and from it there may be much to be learnt about other, less articulate races.

Trade had been vital to Sumer from the first. In the centuries that followed there began an incessant struggle among the various groups of population in Mesopotamia and neighbouring lands for control of the routes. Communications with the north and east, along the river valleys, were particularly difficult to maintain in the face of hostile mountain tribes. To reach the west and the shores of the Mediterranean meant crossing the desert between the Euphrates and Aleppo; after which the easiest route from Syria to the Lebanon, Palestine, and Egypt was by sea. Northern Iraq had a network of routes into Anatolia and across to the east, also endangered by the hill-people. Traders of this period were particularly at a disadvantage in long-distance journeys that entailed a desert crossing; their pack-animals—the ass and donkey—could not go great distances without water, which meant that travel had

to be confined largely to the spring in such areas, when water wa:
still to be found in the waterholes left after the winter rain. The
use of camels, which eased this problem, was not introduced unti
very much later. Security was also a difficulty; the waterholes were
jealously guarded as the prerogative of certain tribes, and the
wandering and marauding clansmen made travel a dangerou:
business except in large well-guarded caravans. Later contracts and
letters amply illustrate the careful administration that went into
the organization of caravan-trading, with references to water
supplies, the licensing of caravan masters, the freedom of certain
caravans to pass through specified areas, and indications of the
precise routes to be followed.

The rivers themselves were utilized as much as possible fo:
transport, but navigation upstream was impracticable north of the
plains because of the rapid current, while downstream it wa
dangerous for the same reason. Both rivers are full of sand-banks
small islands, and other obstacles. A method of transport customary
from ancient times was to float down the Euphrates, which i
slightly more stable than the Tigris, in wooden boats or rafts made
of inflated goat-skins, known as *keleks* and still used today. At Hi
or Deir ez Zor on the Middle Euphrates the craft were dismantled
and carried back upstream. In addition great use was made o
inland waterways, for instance between Lagash and Nippur,
distance of 85 miles; barges had to be towed upstream, which too
over a fortnight; but the return journey took only four or five days
There was also a certain amount of shipping in the Persian Gulf
connecting with the Isle of Bahrein and perhaps the Arabian coast

For merchants undeterred by hardship and risk to life an
property, there was much to be gained in travelling abroad
Gradually private enterprise increased and the city-states lost thei
direct control of the business world. Their rivalries and perpetua
quarrels over boundaries and water-supplies continually sappe
their political strength, and the priesthood had become decadent
Attempts at reform proved fruitless, but at length the rise of Luga
zaggisi of Uruk, about the twenty-fourth century B.C., was dis
tinguished by an invitation to all the principal gods of the souther:
cities to become his patrons. This bid for imperialism, the first of it
kind, was baulked by Sargon of Agade.

For many centuries there had been an infiltration of Semiti
people into Mesopotamia. They were nomadic people migratin,
from the Arabian desert with their flocks, and attracted to th
settled agricultural areas. Their independent traditions did no

make it easy to accept the more despotic system which they encountered in the city-states of Sumer, but the opportunity for
economic prosperity offered advantages. For a long time they kept
up their ancient traditions of pastoral life, living on the fringe of
the Sumerian cities, and gradually settling to the north and north-
west. In the region of modern Baghdad their presence was acknow-
ledged by the name of Akkad. Their appearance as a political force
ended the Early Dynastic period in Sumer.

Sargon was a cup-bearer to the king of Kish, one of the Sumerian
city-states. For the first time in Mesopotamian history we get a
picture of a human being who made a name for himself. He
established himself as king and Agade as his capital:

'Sargon the mighty, King of Akkad am I.
My mother was lowly, my father I knew not,
The brother of my father dwelt in the mountains.
My city is Azupiranu, which lieth on the bank of the Euphrates,
My lowly mother conceived me, in secret she brought me forth,
She cast me into the river, which (rose) not over me.
The river bore me up, unto Akki, the irrigator, it carried me,
Akki the irrigator lifted me out,
Akki the irrigator reared me up,
Akki the irrigator as his gardener appointed me.
When I was his gardener, the goddess Ishtar loved me,
And for fifty-four years I ruled the kingdom,
The black-headed people I ruled, I governed,
The mighty mountains with axes of bronze did I destroy.'

Before finally overcoming the Sumerian army, Sargon made
sure of his supremacy in the north of Mesopotamia, capturing
Mari, Assur, Kirkuk and Arbil. Elam was also subdued, and he
advanced into north Syria and down the Mediterranean coast.
There is an interesting record of his crossing the Taurus and
invading Asia Minor to go to the help of a trading colony of Mesopotamian merchants in Cappadocia, bringing back with him
'specimens of foreign trees, vines, figs and roses for acclimatization
in his own land'. And in Sumer he devoted himself to the rebuilding of temples; at the *ziggurat* in Nippur a simple inscription
stamped on a baked brick was found: 'I, Shar-gali-shari (Sargon),
King of Akkad, have built a temple for Enlil.'

With Sargon's successor, Naram-Sin, came the official introduc-
tion of the title 'King of Sumer and Akkad', which was to be retained throughout the many dynasties of Babylon. The Sargonid

Empire disintegrated after not much more than a century, but its cultural influence remained. The people of Akkad had learnt to write their own Semitic tongue in the Sumerian script. Their long and close association with the older civilization of Sumer had resulted in something highly fertile.

It is very difficult to get much picture of the following two or three centuries. Akkad was overrun by a people 'who knew not kingship', and for a long time there was confusion in the area. But there is evidence that the trading connexions built up by the Akkadian kings were still in operation, particularly in the west, and during the short-lived Sumerian revival that followed, the Semitic flair for commerce became increasingly apparent. Contracts between private individuals were now much more frequent, and large estates became the property of rich merchants who did business on their own account as well as on behalf of the palace or temple. Later, in Larsa, there were even cases of villages or other property being named after the private landowner, a state of affairs which would have been unthinkable in old Sumerian times. In the meantime scribes were engaged on a task that had never been previously attempted. They had begun to record the glories of Sumer over the past thousand years of her history.

With the opening of the second millennium B.C. there was a new influx of Semitic people into Mesopotamia. They came from the west, from the land known as Amurru, where they had established considerable power in Syria and Palestine. We have no reliable chronicle of political events during the period of their installation in the Euphrates region; the history of the Amorites is in fact virtually unknown, though they are thought to have originated in Arabia. But what we do know is that these were the people who founded the First Dynasty of Babylon, and transformed this obscure Akkadian town into a capital city. In doing so they accomplished two things destined to ensure lasting authority. They had chosen a site of strategic importance for the control of trade; and they had chosen an ancient centre of Akkadian worship.

The site of Agade has never been found, but it is believed to have been in the neighbourhood of Babylon, possibly a little farther north. Its history is lost from the time of Sargon, apart from a reference in the Hammurabi period to a temple of Ishtar there; it was probably laid waste by the mountain tribes who overthrew the Sargonid Empire. The rediscovery of Agade might produce a mint of information on Akkadian history. Its position was presumably fairly central, but perhaps less favourably situated than that of

Mari: The Royal Steward Ibhil.

(Third millennium B.C. *Louvre*)

Babylon, which lay across the principal international trading routes. Babylon was in fact a meeting-point; the Euphrates and Tigris linked the city with the west and north, and across to the east lay the third main approach through the Gates of Zagros to Iran. The southern plains were afforded a protection Sumer had never enjoyed, and the city was in a good position to control the inland waterways and coastal traffic. The fact that the vicinity of Babylon has remained an area of choice for the building of capital cities sufficiently demonstrates its strategic and commercial significance, and it was to this that Babylon owed her continuing material prosperity.

But material success, as Hammurabi taught the people of Babylon, was but the corollary of spiritual supremacy. In centralizing the administration of social and economic affairs, in tightening state control on trade and virtually eliminating private profiteering for some time to come, in vesting the conduct of business in the temples where it became largely the province of priestesses, he was following ancient Sumerian tradition. Marduk and Ishtar, the principal deities of Babylon, had been worshipped of old in Akkad. To what extent Semitic gods had been incorporated in the religion of the nomadic pioneers as they settled in Akkad and gradually assimilated Sumerian beliefs we do not know. But the origins of both Marduk and Ishtar can be traced in the religion of Sumer. Babylon had been an Akkadian religious centre; and it is reasonable to suppose that her ancient temple of Marduk, restored by Hammurabi, contained a rich collection of religious documents derived from Sumerian literature and translated into Akkadian, a language already extensively used in commerce and presenting no particular difficulty to the Amorites. The ideas they thus encountered presented a subtle blending of the Sumerian and the Semitic elements: a highly developed culture of great age, linked with creation itself and the gods and kings of pre-Deluge times; and a newer spirit of independence and vigorous enterprise which they themselves could readily share. To the Babylonians the ancient governing principle of order out of chaos had an instant appeal. Practical ingenuity and the will to prosper were in their blood. And to these they added a new ideal, the establishment of justice and equity on earth.

I

THE OLD BABYLONIAN ERA

ON the banks of the Euphrates in Southern Iraq is the site of ancient Babylon, fifty-four miles to the south of Baghdad. Bricks and rubble, a series of mounds and waterlogged hollows, a small museum and a railway halt are its main distinguishing features today. The ruins date from the death of Alexander the Great at Babylon in 323 B.C., when the city was finally abandoned. Wind, sand and water, and centuries of quarrying by villagers, have combined to obliterate what was once the masterpiece of men of genius. And one is reminded of the grim words of the prophet Jeremiah: 'Therefore the wild beasts of the desert shall dwell there . . . and it shall be no more inhabited forever.'

Scenes of desolation such as this are by no means unfamiliar in Mesopotamia. The region of the Tigris and Euphrates abounds in ancient sites; cities of great beauty and renown, such as were admired by Herodotus in their fertile valleys of antiquity, have lain undisturbed for thousands of years beneath the soil. Civilizations were born and flourished here: Sumer, with its principal cities of Uruk, Eridu, Kish, Ur, Mari, Nippur, and Lagash; Akkad, whose city of Agade has never yet been found; the First Dynasty of Babylon; the Kassite Dynasty; Assyria, with its great cities of Khorsabad, Nineveh, Assur, and Calah (Nimrud); and the Neo-Babylonians. The last half of the first millennium B.C. was a period of foreign domination, by Persia, the Seleucid Empire, Parthia, and Rome. Ruins and mounds of rubble remain, but the ancient splendours of Mesopotamia have largely disappeared from the scene. Away from the towns and cultivated areas, a sense of emptiness assails the modern visitor; the flat bare plains are vast expanses of dried mud, criss-crossed here and there by the ancient irrigation canals long since disused. The very beasts of the field seem to have forsaken this wilderness with its burning nightmare of a sky; it has become the realm of snakes and scorpions. In this strange world, where temples were erected long ago to gods of terrifying aspect, where the traveller follows paths that belong to

41

vanished kingdoms and the very silence seems to evoke sounds from the past, it is easy to lose all sense of values and to forget, under the harsh light, what a green plain or river ever looked like.

The old historic desert tracks can still be distinguished to-day. One runs from Ras el Ain in Upper Mesopotamia, where the site of Tell Halaf dates from the earliest settlements in this area, down to Hassetshe, which controlled, on the Habur, a network of ancient highways and caravan routes as far as Nineveh. Another goes south to Deir ez Zor and Mardin from Nisibin, whose streets echoed to the sound of Assurbanipal's chariot wheels, and which the Arab poet Ibn Batuta somewhat extravagantly compared with Damascus for 'the beauty of her gardens and the number of her canals'. Yet another leads from Raqqa, where the disciplined legionaries of Alexander the Great encamped in the shade of the palace, to Dora-Europos, once the frontier of Europe on the Euphrates and the site where Nicanor founded a Macedonian colony. The routes are haunted everywhere by ghosts and memories, ruthless conquerors who came this way in transitory glory, and, on all sides, traces of great empires that collapsed. Where else are so many relics of perished civilizations to be found? All over Mesopotamia, where so much of the land is deserted to-day, kingdoms were established by kings who ruled over territory extending to the shores of the known seas, yet whose names mean little to most of us now. Under the pitiless sun, the cities of long ago lie ruined in the dust, mere tokens of an illustrious past. Yet their relics have borne witness to the cultural influence of societies rich in genius.

Mesopotamian art has told us much about the past; but it is to the documents preserved for thousands of years in rubble and ashes that we chiefly owe our knowledge of the Babylonian and Assyrian way of life. Clay tablets by the thousand and inscriptions upon stone, literary works as well as legal, historical, religious and economic records, attest the struggles and achievements of civilized communities possessing remarkable gifts. Amongst these documents are Babylonian calendars of over three thousand years ago, stating the exact hour of the opening of the gates of the Temple of Marduk; and we can turn up school-children's homework, marriage contracts, and the price of barley, not to mention that of victory, on such tablets as those from Nineveh, many of which are blackened from the fire that ravaged the city when it was finally destroyed. With the help of such material it has been possible gradually to piece together the main events of the period during which Babylon became a city famed throughout the ancient world.

In southern Mesopotamia the historical record goes back some five thousand years. Lagash, one of the earliest city-states of this region, was a thriving community governed by independent princes who sought to improve the lot of their subjects. On the clay tablets of this period there are some interesting details of everyday life. Wages varied, according to type of occupation, its importance and relative usefulness; thus a woman of the harem might receive thirty *qa* of barley a month (about two-thirds of a bushel), and a guardian of asses four times as much. Women who worked also received, apart from their wages, a supplementary sum for each child in their charge. (Family allowances can hardly be described as a modern innovation, since they were a legal right at Lagash in Mesopotamia in the third millennium B.C.) The Sumerians of Lagash were prosperous and contented. They were expert at irrigation and in the preparation of flour from wheat and barley. They lived well on milk bread, turtledove and pomegranates, and their favourite wines came from the mountains of the East or from their own date-palms. Abundant revenue supplied the Public Treasury from temple and palace property, gifts made to the royal children, and dues in the form of cattle, fish, and perfume. The maintenance of the temples, the sacrifices, the funerary and magical rites, were all carried out by the priests; and it appears that the last king of Lagash had to bring in certain drastic reforms in an attempt to stamp out increasing corruption amongst the priests and officials of the city.

The Early Dynastic period in Sumer was brought to a close during the second half of the third millennium B.C. by the rise of the Semitic dynasty of Sargon of Agade: 'Uruk (Erech) was smitten with weapons. Its kingship to Agade was carried. . . .' Akkadian supremacy was to have far-reaching effects. Sargon of Agade was a great ruler whose name passed into legend; he imposed his authority north of the Euphrates and down into Syria and the Lebanon. His grandson, Naram-Sin, was no less illustrious; he was the 'god of Agade', who covered Mesopotamia with temples and palaces, subdued the Elamites, and penetrated into the country of the Guti and as far as Asia Minor. He was the first of the rulers of Sumer and Akkad who took the title 'King of the Four Regions of the World': 'And the journey that no other king among the kings had marched, Naram-Sin the King of Agade marched, and the goddess Innana gave him no rival . . . Naram-Sin the mighty opened a path, and the (Nergal) gave him Aram, Ibla, and presented to him Amanus, the mountains of cedar and the Upper Sea.'

After the death of Naram-Sin the power of Agade waned, Elam regained her independence, and the mountain tribes swarmed down into the valley. In the violence and disruption that followed, the Sargonid dynasty came to an end. But Akkadian speech and institutions had come to stay; the Semitic language had been widely adopted in Mesopotamia and the neighbouring lands, and Akkadian was to become the official language of diplomacy and international trade for many centuries.

Towards the end of the third millennium B.C. there was a remarkable Sumerian revival under the Third Dynasty of Ur which succeeded in driving out the Guti and establishing control over Lower Mesopotamia and the land of Elam. The records we have of this period are mainly religious, but the commercial documents indicate that trade was beginning to flourish. The autonomous city-states became the partners of Ur, jointly and severally responsible for her prosperity. And Ur very soon became great. There was a constant coming and going in and around the city; couriers came from near and far, the river traffic increased, the caravans multiplied. Foreign traders, such as the Martu and the people of Kanesh, were about in large numbers, making money wherever opportunity offered. The plains of Mesopotamia—those same plains which are now for the most part a huge expanse of dried mud—were watered by innumerable canals, carefully maintained. The business accounts of the merchants of Ur of four thousand years ago were drawn up just as ours are to-day, with monthly statements, annual stock-takings, and the careful recordings of receipts, outgoings, and balance.

There is not much evidence of military activity during this period; Ur-nammu, the founder of the dynasty, devoted much of his time to pious works, restoring and rebuilding the temples at several of the important city-states. In addition he rebuilt the royal palace and the city-wall at Ur, and restored the great *ziggurat* tower, the scene of the most sacred Old Sumerian religious ceremonial, and regarded as the link between heaven and earth.

The destruction of Ur in 2016 B.C. put an end to this period of social and economic prosperity in Mesopotamia. The Sumerians were unable to withstand a double onslaught, by Amorites to the north and Elamites to the east. A lament for Sumer was found in the ruins at Nippur:

'When they overthrew, when order they destroyed
 Then like a deluge all things together the Elamite consumed.
 Whereunto, O Sumer, did they change thee?

The sacred dynasty from the temple they exiled
They demolished the city, they demolished the temple,
They seized the rulership of the land. . . .'

It was to be over two hundred years before a new city-state was to achieve comparable stature. With the gradual disintegration of the Sumerian Empire the rulers of Isin and Larsa strove to maintain authority, but the power behind them came from Elam in the Persian plain beyond the Tigris. Here, at the rich capital city of Susa, which had repeatedly been in the hands of foreigners, a strong native dynasty seized the opportunity to expand westwards, and the ferocity of the Elamites became a byword in the land. A later omen-text is significant: 'If the year-star rises with its face towards the west, and looks towards the face of heaven, if no wind blows, there will be famine, and the ruler will meet the fate of Ibi-Sin, King of Ur, who went in bonds to Anshan.'

But by the eighteenth century B.C. a new power was abroad in Mesopotamia. After a long and bitter struggle to preserve their independence the Elamites were forced to yield before the superior might of the First Dynasty of Babylon.

*   *   *

The founding of the First Babylonian Dynasty was the work of the Amorites, a Semitic race known as 'The People of the West'. Babylon, an Akkadian city long since established as a religious centre for the worship of Marduk, rapidly developed into a first-class political power, strongly fortified against pillaging nomads and ambitious neighbouring states. With the accession of Hammurabi, the sixth king of the dynasty, there began the first golden age of Babylon—the second being that of Nebuchadnezzar, over a thousand years later. The systematic unification of Babylonia under the highly centralized government of Hammurabi had no parallel in Mesopotamian history; the old world of Sumer and Akkad, with its petty kingdoms and shifting alliances, where even the calendar varied from one city-state to the next, had lacked the kind of economic organization that can sustain political success. Hammurabi was the first of the great administrators of history, a reformer dedicated to the service of his people: 'Anum and Enlil (the sky and storm gods) named me to promote the welfare of the people, me, Hammurabi, the devout, god-fearing prince, to cause justice to prevail in the land, to destroy the wicked and the evil, that the strong might not oppress the weak, to rise like the sun over the black-headed (people), and to light up the land. Hammurabi, the shepherd, called by Enlil, am I; the one who makes affluence and plenty abound . . . the one, who revived Uruk; who supplied water in abundance to its people;. . . the one who brings joy to Borsippa; . . . who stores up grain for mighty Urash; . . . the saviour of his people from distress, who establishes in security their portion in the midst of Babylon . . . that justice might be dealt the orphan and the widow . . . I established law and justice in the language of the land, thereby promoting the welfare of the people.'

This Prologue to the Code of Hammurabi is indeed an object lesson in political morality. Here we have a body of law drawn up nearly 4,000 years ago to bring about a greater justice in men's dealings one with another, and to improve the lot of those directly concerned with the prosperity of the kingdom. The text is inscribed on a magnificent stele of black diorite, 8 feet high, recovered at Susa in 1902 and now in the Louvre. Above the inscription is a finely sculptured scene in low relief, showing Hammurabi receiving the new Laws from the hands of Shamash, the Sun God, before whose holy presence he vowed to protect the legal rights of his people. In accordance with the artistic convention of the time the god is seated and the worshipper stands before him.

Henceforth, a man who could not pay his debts, and was obliged to sell himself into slavery before a magistrate, was guaranteed his freedom after a period of three years in the service of his creditor. Contracts of any kind had to be properly drawn up and witnessed; if a man gave valuable property into the safekeeping of another 'without witnesses and contracts and they have denied its receipt to him at the place where he made the deposit, that case is not subject to claim'. Fraud and carelessness were sternly punished: 'If a woman wine-seller . . . has made the value of the drink less than that of the grain, they shall prove it against that wine-seller and throw her into the water.' Similarly, 'If a builder constructed a house, but did not make his work strong, with the result that the house which he built collapsed and so has caused the death of the owner of the house, that builder shall be put to death.' And in order, perhaps, to promote efficiency in the medical field: 'If a physician performed a major operation on a seignior with a bronze lancet and has caused the seignior's death, or he opened up the eye-socket of a seignior and has destroyed the seignoir's eye, they shall cut off his hand.' On the other hand: 'If a physician has set a seignior's broken bone, or has healed a sprained tendon, the patient shall give five shekels of silver to the physician.'

In old Sumerian times a wife had no rights of divorce. Hammurabi introduced a number of reforms relating to matrimony; unless unfaithfulness could be proved against her, the wife was now to be presumed chaste and her rights together with those of her children were protected. In the event of adultery illicit lovers were drowned in the Euphrates. But in order to prove that the woman was guilty, the plaintiff was confronted with so many minor points to be established beyond doubt that he was likely to end up by getting lost in a labyrinth of pettifogging detail. The woman, in Babylon, was not regarded as the slave or inferior of a man. On the contrary, and thirty-seven centuries before the West made this discovery, she was considered to be his equal, and enjoyed the same legal rights. Under the reign of Hammurabi at Babylon a woman was legally entitled to lend money, buy or lease property, draw up legacies, and accept or turn down contracts. She could bring legal proceedings and give evidence in court. In the sophisticated society of Babylon, with its essentially commercial outlook, the woman's role was by no means relegated to the background.

Before the time of Hammurabi justice had been largely administered by the priests, 'Judges of the Gates of the Temple'; but the king of Babylon, in order to avoid what he termed 'the abuse of the divine', replaced them by civil judges, palace officials, and local magistrates. This sweeping reform established the rule of law throughout Babylonia and her empire, and made it clear to all concerned that the time of bribes and favours was over, and that justice henceforth would come, not from the god of Sippar or the god of Nippur or the god of Larsa, but from the supreme god of Babylon and the king his servant. A new spirit animated the world. Over 3,500 years before the equality of all citizens before the law was decreed by the French Revolution, this very concept was already laid down in the Code of Hammurabi.

An imaginative passage from the work of the great American historian James Henry Breasted portrays the everyday detail of Hammurabi's work:

'In short clear sentences the king begins dictating his brief letters, conveying his commands to the local governors of the old Sumerian cities which he now rules. The secretary draws a reed stylus from a leathern holder at his girdle, and quickly covers the small clay tablet with its lines of wedge groups. The writer then sprinkles over the soft wet tablet a handful of dry powdered clay. This is to prevent the clay envelope, which he now deftly wraps about the letter, from adhering to the written surface. On this soft envelope he writes the address and sends the letter out to be put into the furnace and baked.

'Messengers constantly hand him similarly closed letters. This secretary of Hammurabi is a trusted confidential clerk. He therefore breaks to pieces the hard clay envelopes in the king's presence and reads aloud to him letters from all over the kingdom. . . . The flood has obstructed the Euphrates between Ur and Larsa, and of course a long string of boats have been tied up and are waiting. The king's reply orders the governor of Larsa to clear the channel at the earliest moment and make it navigable again. . . .

'The calendar has slipped forward a whole month in advance of the proper season, and the king sends out a circular letter to all the governors, saying, "Since the year hath a deficiency, let the month which is now beginning, be registered as a second month of Elul." But he warns the governors that all taxes otherwise falling due within the next month are not to be deferred by this insertion. Delinquent tax-gatherers are firmly reminded of their obligations and called upon to settle without delay. . . .

'The chief of the temple bakers finds that royal orders to look after a religious feast at Ur will call him away from the capital city just at the time when he has an important law-suit coming on. He easily obtains an order from the king postponing the law-suit. The king's interest in the religious feast is here as much concerned as his sense of justice, for many of the letters which he dictates have to do with temple property and temple administration, in which he constantly shows his interest.'

Thus Babylon, under the able government of Hammurabi, became the political capital of the East, the pivot of culture and commerce. The achievements of this remarkable city-state seemed bound to ensure peace and prosperity for its inhabitants for a long time to come. But peace, alas, never seems to last. Friendly relations between peoples have never been known to continue indefinitely. Only a century or so after the death of one of the most dynamic and courageous reformers of history, the clamour of the Hittites, pressing in from Syria, was heard on the borders of the Euphrates.

Invasion brought the inevitable train of disasters. Thriving cities, after a single night of battle, were left for dead. Blood flowed everywhere, and fire raged in all the four quarters of Babylonia. The gods and the demons hid themselves. Corpses by the thousand were borne away by the rivers towards the distant sea. There were

[24] Stele of Hammurabi: Shamash, the Sun-god, presenting Hammurabi King of Babylon, with the Code of Laws. Early second millennium B.C. (*Louvre. A cast of this stele is in the British Museum.*)

[25] Worshipper before Shamash, the Sun-god. Early second millennium B.C. (*Louvre.*)

[26] A Babylonian treatise on astronomy. This tablet is inscribed with classified lists of the principal stars and constellations, heliacal risings and settings, culminations in the south, etc. Although this is a fairly late text (about the sixth century B.C.) much of this astronomical work was based on observations dating from the time of Hammurabi, about twelve centuries earlier. (*British Museum.*)

[27] Two views of a clay model
of a sheep's liver. The surface is
divided up and labelled for purposes of divination. (*British
Museum.*)

[28] Figure of a deity, possibly of Hurrian origin. In bronze, silver-plated; early second millennium B.C. (*Louvre.*)

Syrian deity in bronze: probably second millennium B.C. (*Louvre.*)

[30] Tell Ahmar: Stele of the god Teshup. The
Hittite deity is shown armed with the thunderbolt
and axe. Second millennium B.C. (*Louvre.*)

[31] Tell Ahmar: The goddess Ishtar on the back of a lion, her sacred animal. (*Louvre.*)

] Susa: Boundary-stone of Nazi-
ruttash. Fourteenth century B.C.
ouvre.)

[32] Kassite boundary-stone from second millennium B.C. Stele depicting Babylonian
pantheon. 'The divine emblems are arranged in five registers, starting at the top and
reading from left to right. *First register:* At the top of the stele, the crescent: SIN;
eight-pointed star: ISHTAR; solar disc: SHAMASH; beneath, in the same register, are two
altars, side by side, each with a horned crown: ANU and ENLIL; the next altar, with the
goat-fish and ram in conjunction, symbolizes EA; the fourth emblem is difficult to
identify. If interpreted as the umbilical cord with the knife used to sever it, this could
be the altar of the Mother-Goddess, possibly NINHURSAG, who presided over confine-
ments. *Second register:* Three deities of war are shown: NERGAL, with the winged lion
and panther jaws; the vulture and curved weapon of ZABABA (?); and the griffin and
curved weapon of NINURTA (?). *Third register:* These figures are easier to identify:
MARDUK is represented by his dragon and the *marru* or triangular tool; NABU, the
scribal deity, can be recognized by the tablet and writing implement on the altar; and
it is clearly GULA who is guarded by the sacred hound. *Fourth register:* The bull and
altar with thunderbolt represent ADAD, but it is difficult to say which deity is symbolized
by the ram and chisel (?) which follow; the lamp, however, suggests NUSKU, and the
plough, NINGIRSU; the bird perched on a post is that of SHUQAMUNA, a Kassite deity.
The other bird possibly represents SHIMALIYA (?), the divine consort. *Fifth register:*
If there is a sheaf on the altar at the left, this may represent NISABA, originally a corn-
goddess. The scorpion is certainly the emblem of ISHARA. As for the horned serpent,
this probably indicates NINGIZZIDA.' (*André Parrot. Louvre.*)

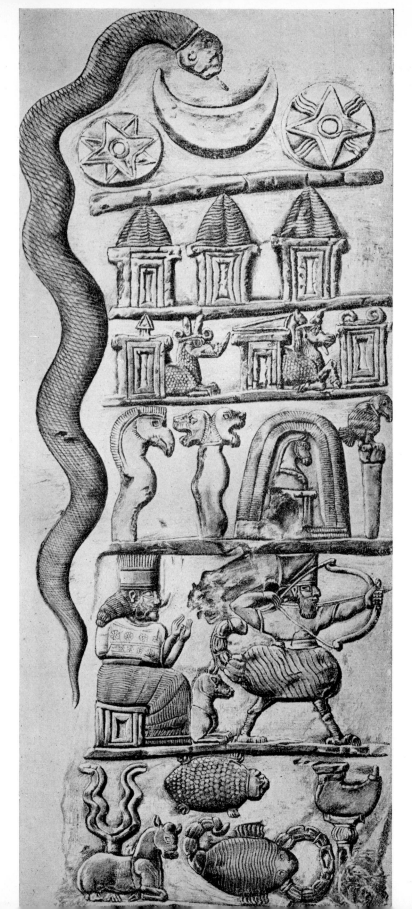

[35] Susa: Boundary-stone of the Kassite King Melishipak II: twelfth century B.C. (*Louvre*.)

[3
m
S
tu

[34] Limestone stele of Nebuchadnezzar I, King of Babylon in the twelfth century B.C. This stele records the royal bestowal of privilege on Ritti-Marduk, a governor of the district bordering on Elam, in recognition of his bravery. Many of the deities belonging to the Babylonian pantheon are represented here by their sacred emblems. (*British Museum*.)

[40] Head of a deity, from North Syria; ? first millennium B.C. (*Louvre.*)

[41] The Gates of Shalmaneser III: Ninth century B.C. (*above*) The King of Assyria arriving to lay siege to a city.
[42] (*below*) The King is installed before the besieged city. (*British Museum.*)

[43] The Gates of Shalmaneser III: Ninth century B.C. (*above*) Exchange of congratulations and military exercises before a campaign.

[44] (*below*) Archers attacking a Mesopotamian citadel. (*British Museum*.)

[45] The Gates of Shalmaneser III: Ninth century B.C. (*above*) The Assyrian archers bear themselves nobly.

[46] (*below*) The army leaving their entrenchment. Standard-bearers can be seen riding in the chariots. (*British Museum.*)

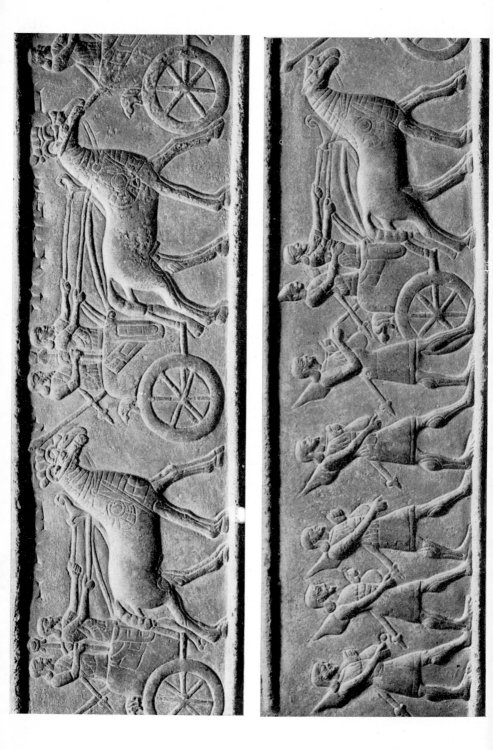

[49] Assyrian relief: In the besieged fortress the defenders await the onslaught of the enemy. (*Louvre.*)

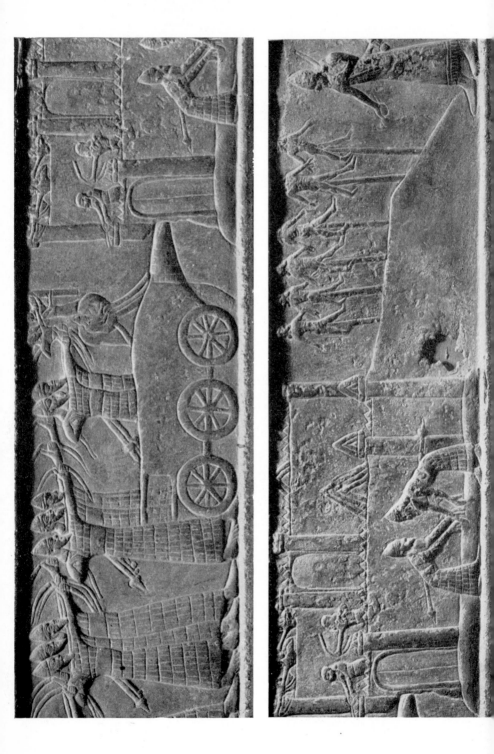

[52] The Gates of Shalmaneser III: Ninth century B.C. (*above*) Homage to the King.

[53] (*below*) Bringers of tribute arriving by boat. (*British Museum.*)

Prisoners of War, bound together in pairs. From an Assyrian relief. (*Louvre.*)

[55] Envoys from vassal states bringing tribute. (*British Museum.*)

[56] Nimrud: Detail from Obelisk of Shalmaneser III. Jehu bows down before the King of Assyria and offers silver, gold, lead, and precious vessels as tribute. In the centre sacred emblems are depicted. (*British Museum.*)

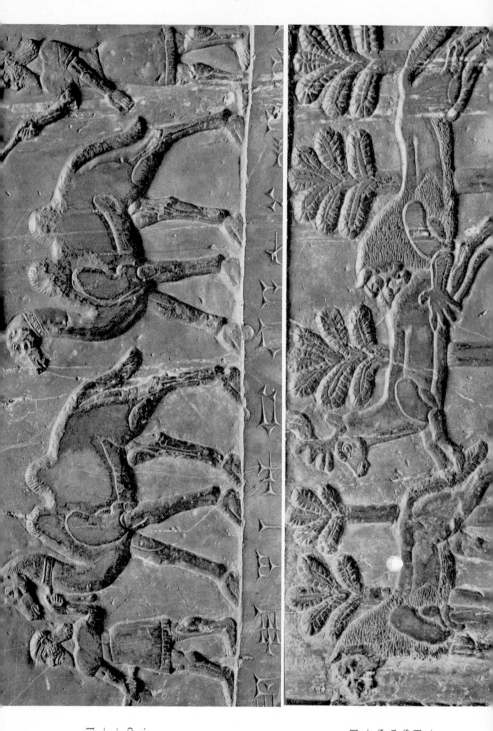

[57] Nimrud: Detail from Obelisk of Shalmaneser III. Dromedaries brought to the king as tribute. (*British Museum.*)

[58] Nimrud: Detail from Obelisk of Shalmaneser III. Lions after their prey in the mountain forests of Sukhu, a vassal state. (*British Museum.*)

Bas-relief of As-
griffin-demon.
figure has also been
preted as that of a
wearing winged
el and a bird-
d mask. Ninth-
century B.C.
re.)

[60] Head of winged genius from Assyria: Ninth century B.C. (*Louvre.*)

[61] Bas-relief from Nimrud: Bearers of tribute in the form of apes from distant lands,
s an offering to the Assyrian ruler. Ninth century B.C. (*British Museum.*)

[62–*overleaf*] Assyrian protective winged genius. Ninth century B.C. (*Louvre.*)

iots, violations, deportations, and the uprooting of whole popu-
ations. (The fall of the First Babylonian Empire heralded the end
f this phase of civilization in the region for several centuries.

But a time came eventually when dynastic rule began to be re-
stablished at Babylon, this time under the Kassite kings. The city
tself had been relatively spared during this lengthy period of
evastation and upheaval. The Kassites, a dynasty of Indo-Iranian
rigin, were mountain people from the Zagros region, attracted
y all the rich enticements of the fertile plains which they had
vithin bowshot. Their domination was destined to last for several
uundred years, the longest foreign conquest known in Meso-
otamia.

During this period there is a long gap in the annals of Baby-
onia. When continuous records reappear, it is apparent that the
cene had changed considerably. By this time the power of the
Iittites was on the wane; but a new, young, and vigorous empire
ad arisen in Assyria and was pressing southward upon Babylon.

II

THE ASSYRIAN EMPIRE

As the fortunes of Babylon steadily declined, Assyria became a
increasing source of danger in the north, her influence very soo
replacing that of her rival in the Tigris-Euphrates region and a
far as the shores of Lake Van. Egypt, after a trial of strength wit
the Hittites, was beginning to lose grip on her empire. There was
temporary revival in Elam, resulting in the final overthrow of th
Kassites, and a new dynasty in Babylon under Nebuchadnezzar
succeeded for a short time in regaining independence; but onc
again Elam was to disappear from the political scene at the hands o
the Babylonians, who themselves were doomed to many centurie
of strife and vassalage.

Assyria rose swiftly to fame. The successful campaigns o
Tiglath Pileser I towards the end of the twelfth century B.C. ha
brought in a wealth of tribute to the royal city of Assur. But it wa
some three hundred years before Assyria achieved the coveted supre
macy. For the best part of this period the Aramaeans in Syria suc
ceeded in keeping her at bay; but early in the ninth century B.C.
with the advent of Assur-nasir-pal II, the military genius o
Assyria took the ancient world by storm, and a long succession o
merciless conquerors laid waste the land.

Nimrud (Calah) now became the Assyrian capital, its roya
palace decorated with elegant carvings in bas-relief and hug
sculptured figures. The campaigns of Shalmaneser III, the sor
of Assur-nasir-pal, who overran both Syria and Babylonia, wer
recorded upon his famous gates of bronze, now in the Britisl
Museum. On a black stone obelisk found at Nimrud scenes depict
ing the payment of tribute to Shalmaneser indicate the rapi
spread of the empire. The period following his death was tem
porarily one of slight setback for Assyria, with revolts in Syria an
Babylon. A total eclipse of the sun in 763 B.C. was interpreted as a
sign of divine wrath and there were civil disturbances in Nimrud
culminating in the seizure of the throne by an Assyrian genera
who took the name Tiglath-Pileser. Under his leadership Assyri

resumed her policy of conquest and wholesale deportations of population. Transported in state to Babylon, twelve months before his death, Tiglath-Pileser took the ancient title, 'King of Sumer and Akkad'.

His successor was murdered, and another usurper took the throne in the name of Sargon II; thus was the great Sargon of Agade commemorated by a military prodigy. The yearly campaigns went on with undiminished success and ferocity: 'I, Sargon, king of the four regions (of the world), ruler (shepherd) of Assyria, . . . who carefully observes the law of Shamash, of the stock of Assur, the city of learning, quick of wit, who waits reverently upon the word of the great gods, never violating their ordinances; I, Sargon, the rightful king, whose words are gracious, whose abomination is falsehood, from whose mouth (words) bringing evil and harm do not emanate; most wise prince of the regions (of the earth), who was created in wisdom and understanding, who sustains the fear of the gods and goddesses; to Assur, king of all the great gods, lord of the lands, creator of (prophetic) vision, king of the totality of the great gods, who illumines the regions (of the earth) . . . because I had never yet come near Ursâ, the Armenian, and the border of his wide land, nor poured out the blood of his warriors on the (battle)-field, I lifted my hands, praying that I might bring about his defeat in battle, turn his innocent words against himself, and make him bear his sin. . . .'

The reign of this monarch, who so effectively displayed his hackneyed titles on the granite stelae designed to perpetuate the memory of his race, may be said to have attained the zenith of Assyrian greatness. In having himself crowned at Babylon—a move which demonstrates his political acumen—Sargon added cultural brilliance to his position of military supremacy. Although Babylon was no longer the political and commercial centre of Western Asia, she had retained a spiritual and religious significance throughout this period in spite of constant wars and alarms. Babylon was irreplaceable.

Once again there was a shift of capital. The new Assyrian city built by Sargon at Khorsabad was on a monumental scale, with mud-brick walls over seventy-five feet thick and huge ornamental gateways with colossal figures sculptured in stone. Inside the palace the vast expanse of the walls was covered with carvings in bas-relief, depicting scenes from Sargon's victorious campaigns, processions and religious ceremonies, and strange magical figures symbolizing the protective genius of the king.

Sargon did not live long to enjoy his fantastic city. Barely tw
years after his formal entry into Khorsabad he was assassinated i
705 B.C.

Sennacherib, his son, chose Nineveh as his capital. A prodigiou
amount of labour went into improving, enlarging, and embellish
ing the palace and city. Parks and gardens were laid out an
planted with trees and flowers native to distant lands now unde
his dominion. Mountain streams were diverted to Nineveh b
specially constructed canals. Breasted describes the building of th
palace: 'Gold, silver, copper, red sandstone, breccia, alabaster
ivory, maple, box, mulberry, cedar, cypress, pine, olive, oak, all ha
their place in its ornamentation. Within was the bright ename
of glazed brick panels, ceilings white-washed to remove the gloom
and curtains draped back across elaborate silver bosses. Near th
doors were colossal cows of marble and ivory bearing up the flower
like calyx on which rested the columns. Winged lions and bull
were cast in bronze for the same purpose and the cedar column
above them were encased in copper. Thus "The Palace without
Rival" was created, the centre of the civilized world.'

But Sennacherib was yet another of this race of conquerors wh
lusted after glory and were unable to tolerate a rival. With fire an
bloodshed he ravaged the land of Judah and went so far as t
besiege Jerusalem. Assyria, at this period, inspired universal hatre
and was attacked on every side. Sennacherib, who was in the habi
of nailing his prisoners to the gates of his palace, sacked, pillaged
and burned in vain. His enemies hammered away at him, surging
up in hordes from every direction to molest and harry him. I
Jerusalem he had Hezekiah shut up 'like a bird in a cage' an
insulted him before his own people in the public square. H
crushed a coalition of the Elamite provinces and the Babyloniar
Empire and proceeded to take his revenge upon the city of Babylon
which, through a combination of bad strategy and the pressure o
events, had inadvertently become the centre of an open insurrec
tion against Nineveh. Babylon must cease to exist, she must vanisl
without trace. Sennacherib gave the gruesome order to take the city
and sack it utterly. And Babylon was taken and sacked. On the
Bavian rock, at the source of the spring which fed the canals o
Nineveh, there appears this account by the ferocious Assyrian
'The city and (its) houses, from its foundation to its top, I destroyed
I devastated, I burned with fire. The wall and the outer wall,
temples and gods, temple towers of brick and earth, as many a
there were, I razed and dumped them into the Arakhtu Canal.

Through the midst of that city I dug canals, I flooded its site with water, and the very foundations thereof I destroyed. I made its destruction more complete than that by a flood. That in days to come the site of that city, and (its) temples and gods, might not be remembered, I completely blotted it out with (floods) of water and made it like a meadow.'

The jealous Ninevite made no attempt to conceal his glee at the spectacle of a great city crumbling in the last red glow of a thousand fires. But the lightning destruction of this sacred site was mourned by all the people of the East. The magnitude of the event was such that when it came to be recorded in the later chronicles no comment was necessary: 'In the first month of Kislev, Babylon was taken, and her king, Mushezib-Marduk, was captured and led away to Assyria.'

But the will of the gods was inscrutable. Some years later, when the city was beginning to rise up once more from the ruins, Sennacherib was murdered: 'And it came to pass, as he was worshipping in the house of his god, that Adrammelech and Sharezer his sons smote him with the sword: and they escaped into the land of Armenia. And Esarhaddon his son reigned in his stead.'

Sennacherib sought to wipe out a city from the face of the earth, by massacre, fire, and wholesale destruction. If his wandering outcast of a ghost were to revisit the scene of his exploits now, it might well seem that it was hardly worth the trouble to go to such lengths for the sake of a fame which has done him little credit. For the wind and the sand have blotted out Babylon far more effectively than he, for all his ruthlessness.

After the murder of Sennacherib the Assyrian Empire slowly diminished in power. The new king, Esarhaddon, 'first among all princes, object of Queen Ishtar's affection, heart's desire of the great gods', was confronted by a situation which was getting rapidly out of hand. Fire smouldered everywhere: in Phoenicia, where Sidon was razed to the ground, in Babylonia, and on the frontiers of Egypt. The tablets of the priests are eloquent: 'Fear not, Esarhaddon! I, the god Bel, speak to you. . . . The god Sin is at your right, the god Shamash at your left; sixty great gods stand round about you, ranged for battle. . . .'

These, the oracle tablets, recording the decrees of Assur, were sprinkled with good oil and carried before the king before the start of a campaign. In one fell swoop the Assyrian went straight from the Euphrates to the Nile, crossing the tribes of the desert, and he took Memphis from the rear: 'Memphis . . . in half a day, with mines, tunnel, assaults, I besieged, I captured, I destroyed, I devastated, I burned with fire.'

Thus fell the most ancient of the great Egyptian cities, founded, according to Herodotus, by Menes, when the Lands of Upper and Lower Egypt were first united, the famous capital of the Old Kingdom. Later, for a short time, the Egyptians succeeded in recapturing their city, only to suffer an even worse defeat at the hands of Assurbanipal.

But in other fields Esarhaddon proved more conciliatory than his predecessors, winning the allegiance of Babylon by his restoration of the city which his father had laid waste. This was a piece of diplomacy well worth while, since he did not have to expend his forces on the defence of Babylonia against marauders from the south and east.

His son, Assurbanipal, is chiefly famous for his annihilation of Thebes in the course of a second Assyrian campaign against Egypt in 669 B.C. and yet another seven years later. He sacked this city of priests with such ferocity—the same savage spirit that had incited Sennacherib to raze Babylon—that the devastation has long served as the perfect model in taking reprisals against a city. 'In my second campaign I made straight for Egypt and Ethiopia. Tandamanê (Pharaoh) heard of the advance of my army and that I was invading the territory of Egypt. He forsook Memphis and fled to Ni' (Thebes) to save his life. The kings, prefects, governors, whom I had installed in Egypt, came to meet me and kissed my feet. I took the road after Tandamanê, marched as far as Ni', his stronghold. . . . That city (Thebes) my hands captured in its entirety,—with the aid of Assur and Ishtar. Silver, gold, precious stones, the goods of his palace, all there was, brightly coloured and linen garments, great horses, the people, male and female, two tall obelisks . . . which stood by the gate of the temple, I removed from their positions and carried them off to Assyria.'

Such is the bald official account of the taking of Thebes; the scenes of carnage and devastation are left to the imagination.

The Library of Assurbanipal, which is preserved at the British Museum, consists of many thousands of tablets, many of which bear distinct traces of the burning of Nineveh. It is the largest and most important collection of Sumerian, Akkadian, Assyrian and Babylonian texts ever discovered beneath the dusty plains of Mesopotamia. As a field of study for the historian it is unique, an invaluable body of information on the history of the East in all its essentials from earliest times up to the fall of the Assyrian Empire. 'This Library', writes Charles-F. Jean, 'contains an entire historical literature. Sometimes the scribes copied out their documents word for word; sometimes they translated them and added short explanatory notes to assist the artist whose task it was to recount the history of their kings on the bas-reliefs, frontier boundary-stones, statues and chariots. Important texts have been deciphered, such as the *Chronicle of the First Kings of Babylon*.'

For the most part the documents from this library are concerned with astrology, medicine and religion. They are highly instructive and have made it possible to understand much more about the history and everyday life of the early civilized communities. They tell us for instance how the people of Mesopotamia used to interpret the omens they continually saw in everything around them, in the sky, in the belly of an animal that had been sacrificed, in monstrous imaginary shapes of all kinds, in the tail of a meteor or the path of lightning. The divinators watched the moon, stately and ever-changing in the clear Assyrian night. In the mingling of the winds they could recognize the sound of 'the gods who howled'; they could assure good fortune to one and all according to the position of Saturn in relation to the halo of the moon. There are thousands of texts recording the observations and interpretations by the Omen-Priests of phenomena of all kinds. Other tablets are enlightening on the lore of the professional magician, who had many skills. He could drive out evil spirits and all hidden corruption from the body of the sufferer; ward off, with ritual formulae, the afflictions which rob a man's body of life; seek out that which is evil wherever it is in hiding, and destroy it by means of sympathetic magic; identify spectres deprived of a burial-place and of funerary offerings and libations; and transform by magical means the monstrous *alù* which has no mouth and no ears and which wanders about in the streets. It was he who hung about the necks of the sick the perforated *pazuzu* heads, the customary precaution, and who could fashion little figurines out of bitumen or crushed sesame for use in sympathetic magic; for whom the future could be seen imprinted upon the entrails or the liver of a sacrificial victim; and who could interpret the behaviour of drops of oil thrown into a bucket of water.

Amongst all the many thousands of tablets from Assurbanipal's Library there is also a selection of hymns and prayers and numerous ritual and ceremonial texts which are informative on the social

and religious beliefs and practices of these ancient peoples. One
of the prayers appears to be addressed to all gods, known and unknown:

> '. . . O Lord, my transgressions are many; great are my sins.
> . . . O god whom I know or do not know, (my) transgressions
> are many; great are (my) sins.
> . . . The god whom I know or do not know has oppressed me;
> The goddess whom I know or do not know has placed suffering
> upon me;
> Although I am constantly looking for help, no one takes me by
> the hand;
> When I weep they do not come to my side.
> I utter laments, but no one hears me;
> I am troubled, I am overwhelmed, I cannot see.
> . . . How long, O my goddess, whom I know or do not know,
> ere thy hostile heart be quieted?
> Man is dumb; he knows nothing;
> Mankind, everyone that exists,—what does he know?
> Whether he is committing sin or doing good, he does not know;
> O my lord, do not cast thy servant down;
> He is plunged into the waters of a swamp; take him by the hand.
> The sin, which I have done, turn into goodness;
> . . . My many misdeeds, strip off like a garment . . .'

The mood of melancholy is characteristic of much of the
literature of Babylon and Assyria. A sidelight on Assurbanipal is
disclosed by a sarcastic letter he wrote to the Babylonians quoting
two proverbs: 'When the potter's dog went into the oven, he
even growled at the potter'; and: 'A sinful woman at the gate of a
judge's house—her word prevails over that of her husband.'

Assurbanipal had sacked Thebes. When he conquered Babylon,
in 648 B.C., he also set fire to Susa and massacred her inhabitants.
'They carried off to Nineveh', writes Charles-F. Jean, 'as was their
custom, gods and goddesses, with all their treasure and religious
officials, the statues of earlier kings, even the sacred bulls which
guarded the temples, and all manner of trophies. They violated the
sepulchres of the kings to deprive them of eternal rest.' And
in the words of Assurbanipal himself:

'The sepulchres of these earlier and later kings . . . I destroyed,
I devastated, I exposed to the sun. Their bones I carried off to
Assyria. I laid restlessness upon their shades. I deprived them of
food offerings and libations of water.'

Susa: Winged Griffin.

(First millennium B.C. *Louvre*)

Assurbanipal was the beloved of the gods of Assur; the son of the Lydian king Gyges begged him to let him carry his yoke. (The Arabs, whose lands were being continually raided by his armies, were decimated by his attentions and were eventually obliged, so far as one can gather from the records, 'to eat the flesh of their children in order to satisfy their hunger.' Selected captives were treated with special favour; one of these, U-a-ate by name, was captured and taken to Nineveh. Assurbanipal received him and smashed his jaw with 'the knife which he was holding in his hand'; after which gesture of welcome he put a cord round his neck, attached him to a dog-leash, and kept him in a kennel. The official accounts of the atrocities become tedious after a time: 'I took him alive, in the midst of battle. In Nineveh, my capital, I slowly tore off his skin.'

But cruelty brought its own reward. Within a few years the sadistic Assyrian had become the most hated and the most feared of the monarchs of the eastern world. His supremacy extended to the limits of the known world. Under his rule a policy of mass deportations and terrorization was pursued, and his repeated prayers to the goddess Ishtar were followed by triumph again and again; but towards the end his grip on the empire began to weaken. Assyria was on the eve of her collapse.)

III

THE NEO-BABYLONIANS

IN the course of the troubled decades that followed the death of
Assurbanipal, life began anew for Babylon. The later chronicles
relate how Assyria was defeated at her last attempt to keep a hold
on Babylonia in 626 B.C. One Babylonian city, possibly Nippur,
which was held by an Assyrian garrison, was besieged so long by the
Babylonian army that the inhabitants had to sell their children for
food. In accordance with military tradition, the gods of Elam had
been borne away in triumph by the Assyrians and deposited at
Uruk; now they were restored to Susa by the astute Nabopolassar,
King of Babylon and founder of a new and brilliant dynasty. By
615 B.C. the Medes under Cyaxares were moving across into Assyria,
where they joined forces with the Babylonians in an alliance that
was to have a profound significance for the future of Babylon.
Three years later, after a three-month siege, Nineveh succumbed
before a tremendous onslaught and the Assyrian Empire came to
an end.

The fall of Nineveh, eclipsed in the smoke of an unforgettable
conflagration, was the signal for plunder by peoples long sup-
pressed, for violation, greed and revenge. It was an event which
rocked the ancient world; but there was more to come. For it was
now the son of Nabopolassar who rode at the head of the Babylonian
army while his father remained in Babylon, a prince whose name
was Nebuchadnezzar, and whose destiny was to go by no means
unnoticed.

Nebuchadnezzar. . . . An extraordinary person if ever there
was one, if one ventures to study him closely. He was old enough to
be well aware of the former might and extraordinary savagery of
the Assyrian kings, and in his youth he had witnessed the flames
that licked the walls of Nineveh, consuming her palaces and
temples and blackening the historic stone reliefs and monuments.
The destruction of that formidable city of splendour, carried off
as if by the wind, made a lasting impression upon his mind.
Nineveh was buried under a heap of ashes; her arrogant warrior-

people had been driven off to the bottom of Nergal's netherworld, where each newcomer receives as his only sustenance the sixty sicknesses that are to afflict him throughout eternity, where he becomes but one more spectre among the drifting shadows, dreaming forever of a return to earth to devour the living. Nineveh was at last exterminated with the help of an obscure Mede, and her Empire was there for the taking. Nebuchadnezzar made the most of his opportunity.

His military career began with a brilliant victory. At the Battle of Carchemish he confronted Egypt, the old enemy with a common purpose—the control of Syria. The rout of the Egyptian army was followed by hot pursuit of the remnants, and according to the Chronicles, 'not a man escaped to his own country'. The historian Josephus records the outcome in a single sentence: 'So the king of Babylon passed over Euphrates and took all Syria, as far as Pelusium, excepting Judea.'

Jehoiakim, King of Judah, had been a vassal of the Egyptian king. He now submitted voluntarily to Nebuchadnezzar, who carried off Jewish captives, including the prophet Daniel, to Babylon.

Nebuchadnezzar's advance was halted at Pelusium; for, according to Berossus: 'Now it so fell out, that his father Nabopolassar fell into a distemper at this time, and died in the city of Babylon, after he had reigned twenty-nine years. But as Nebuchadnezzar understood in a little time, that his father Nabopolassar was dead, he set the affairs of Egypt and other countries in order, and committed the captives he had taken . . . to some of his friends, that they might conduct that part of the forces that had on heavy armour, with the rest of his baggage, to Babylonia; while he went in haste, having but few with him, over the desert to Babylon; whither when he was come, he found the public affairs had been managed by the Chaldeans, and that the principal person among them had preserved the kingdom for him. Accordingly he now entirely obtained all his father's dominions. He then came and ordered the captives to be placed in colonies in the most proper places of Babylonia.'

On the same day that he reached Babylon, the first day of Elul (6th/7th September) 605 B.C., Nebuchadnezzar II ascended the throne. His haste in returning to Babylon by the shortest desert route suggests there was some reason to fear dishonest intriguers; probably his father had not taken the throne without opposition.

War, in the ancient world, was usually conducted in a series of annual campaigns which took place during the summer and autumn months. A period of peace, that is to say an absence of campaigns for several years on end, was exceedingly rare. During the Assyrian domination peace was more or less non-existent; it was always necessary either to subdue revolts or, as a point of honour, to lead out the armies over the already vanquished lands in order to display their military might and collect spoil and tribute. Sometimes, of course, it was a question of fresh conquests in hitherto unexplored territory. Invasion year after year, accompanied by plunder and devastation, and the taking of thousands of prisoners, makes it almost unbelievable that certain scattered kingdoms should somehow have managed to survive in the region between the Euphrates and the Nile.

The Chronicles concerning the reign of Nebuchadnezzar indicate that he followed the traditional pattern, at least at first. The same autumn that he acceded to the throne found him in Syria, consolidating his triumphs and receiving tribute. In the following year he 'marched about unopposed' in Syria, and is recorded as having received tribute from Palestine, possibly from Damascus, Tyre, and Sidon. Annual expeditions followed; there was trouble with the nomadic tribes of the Western Syrian Desert, whom Nebuchadnezzar sought to subdue in the Assyrian manner by removing their gods. A clash with Egypt in 601 B.C. brought 'heavy losses' to both sides, and it appears that Nebuchadnezzar found himself deficient in chariots and horses as a result. He made no further inroads upon Egypt for a considerable time after this setback.

But the Babylonian hurricane was to break once more over Palestine. Jehoiakim, King of Judah, had sworn an oath of fealty for three years, at the end of which time he decided to rebel against Nebuchadnezzar, despite the warnings of Jeremiah: 'Woe unto thee, O Jerusalem! Wilt thou not be made clean? when shall it once be? . . . Therefore saith the Lord: Behold, I will give this city into the hands of the Chaldeans, and into the hand of Nebuchadnezzar, King of Babylon, and he shall take it; And the Chaldeans, that fight against this city, shall come and set fire on this city, and burn it with the houses, upon whose roofs they have offered incense unto Ba'al.'

There are varying accounts of the capture of Jerusalem by Nebuchadnezzar. According to the Babylonian Chronicles, Jehoiakim died shortly before the city was taken; his son, Jehoiachin, was taken prisoner and a substitute, Zedekiah, was appointed in his place by Nebuchadnezzar. Heavy tribute was exacted, but at this point the city was relatively spared. In the royal quarters at Babylon tablets were found giving lists of rations for Jehoiachin and other Jewish captives. But a revolt by Zedekiah ended in disaster for Jerusalem, which according to the Hebrew chroniclers was burnt down:

'Then the king of Babylon slew the sons of Zedekiah in Riblah before his eyes: also the king of Babylon slew all the nobles of Judah.

'Moreover he put out Zedekiah's eyes, and bound him with chains, to carry him away to Babylon.

'And the Chaldeans burned the king's house, and the houses of the people, with fire, and brake down the walls of Jerusalem.

'Then Nebuzar-adan the captain of the guard carried away captive into Babylon the remnant of the people that remained in the city, and those that fell away, that fell to him, with the rest of the people that remained.'

The account given by Josephus gives a different slant to the story. He suggests that Nebuchadnezzar came in person, and 'slew such as were in the flower of their age', including King Jehoiakim, whom he had 'thrown before the walls without burial'. He represents the son Jehoiachin as 'of a gentle and just disposition', who, when Nebuchadnezzar besieged the city, preferred to surrender his mother and family rather than endanger Jerusalem. This, according to Josephus, was done on the understanding that no harm should come to them; but the King of Babylon did not keep his agreement, and he took all the youth and craftsmen of the city as well as Jehoiachin and his mother and friends, into captivity.

Such was the purification of Jerusalem by Babylon, by fire and the sword. Listen to the passionate lamentation of the Psalm of Asaph:

'O God, the heathen are come into thine inheritance; thy holy temple have they defiled; they have laid Jerusalem on heaps.

'The dead bodies of thy servants have they given to be meat unto the fowls of the heaven, the flesh of thy saints unto the beasts of the earth.

'Their blood have they shed like water round about Jerusalem; and there was none to bury them.'

The Babylonians became inflamed with their triumphs and their booty, their violations, massacres, and the stench of blood and fire. In the cindered alleyways they picked on victims at random and set upon them, tearing them apart as if they were indulging in some macabre kind of sport, skinning them alive for the pleasure of showing how well they could do it, scalping and crucifying them in order to savour their victory. With Judah tortured upon the rack, Nebuchadnezzar was able to bow down before the inscrutable Ishtar, Goddess of War; while Jeremiah, that great herald of catastrophes, who had escaped from this unforgettable carnage, was left to lament and thunder his imprecations: 'How doth the city sit solitary, she that was full of people! how is she become as a widow! she that was great among the nations, and princess among the provinces, how is she become tributary!'

Judah was paying the price of pride; she had loved her city too well. And now she was in chains, mocked, abused, and led away into captivity to Babylon to set the final touch to the triumph of her conquerors. Her song of lament would be heard in the 'City of the gods', the city of terrifying aspect with its fabulous beasts and gilded monuments. There amid scenes of rejoicing the long line of captives would move slowly up the steep ascent into the city, to the sound of harps and tambourines, through one gateway after another of the great encircling walls with their brilliant colouring; and the Hebrews halted on the Great Processional Way would glimpse the sacred person of Nebuchadnezzar, eldest son of the Great Lord Marduk, motionless on his chariot amidst the wild acclamations of his people. But a day of deliverance would come:

'By the rivers of Babylon, there we sat down, yea, we wept, when we remembered Zion. . . . If I forget thee, O Jerusalem, let my right hand forget her cunning. . . . O daughter of Babylon, who art to be destroyed; happy shall he be, that rewardeth thee as thou hast served us.'

From this time on there is a long gap in the Babylonian Chronicles, which give us (as yet) no further information about the remaining thirty-three years of Nebuchadnezzar's reign. References to his numerous successful campaigns crop up in other sources, but from the enormous number of building inscriptions and bricks stamped with his name found all over southern Mesopotamia it seems that Nebuchadnezzar devoted much of his time to the work of building and restoring temples, palaces, and fortifications on a scale that surpassed even that of his Assyrian predecessors. Babylon grew in beauty and splendour and was an object of wonder and awe throughout the ancient world.

Nebuchadnezzar realized the importance of the Euphrates as a commercial factor, and made the fullest possible use of the river

by an ingenious reconstruction of the network for navigation and
irrigation much as it was originally laid out some twelve centuries
earlier under the First Babylonian Empire. He dug a long supply
canal, the Libil-higalla, to divert the course of the river, controlled
by an immense artificial basin about forty feet deep which could
be opened or closed by means of sluices. Berossus, who is generally
a reliable source, records that this basin acted as a reservoir for the
waters of the Euphrates, so that water in abundance could be
readily available as required. Without the innumerable canals
dug by the Babylonians Mesopotamia could never have become in
ancient times the granary of the Orient. The capital itself was
greatly extended in the time of Nebuchadnezzar, and surrounded
with a new defensive wall of immense thickness. The royal citadel
was enlarged and a new palace constructed in magnificent style.
Gold, silver and precious stones were lavishly employed to embellish the temples; and the newly-paved Processional Way was
adorned, as was the beautiful Gate of Ishtar, with sacred animals
in brightly-coloured enamelled brick relief.

Never had Babylonian prosperity seemed more assured. Caravans streamed towards the city over every desert route. The
economic imperialism of Nebuchadnezzar encouraged the natural
commercial ability of the townspeople. Merchants began to
exchange pipe-dreams behind their shutters, amassing imaginary
fortunes from the pearls of the Red Sea coast, or the emeralds of
the Gobi picked up by nomadic horsemen at the season of the north
winds. They urged on their caravan masters as far as India, right
into the heart of that kingdom of legend whose reputation for so
many centuries had dazzled earlier kings. Babylon had no rival.
This city of a million inhabitants became the first great commercial centre of the world.

To protect the rights of his subjects and ensure the safety of his
caravans, Nebuchadnezzar, who was nothing if not an innovator,
conceived the idea of building amid the stony desert of Arabia a
new capital, where all the products of the world could be stored in
gigantic warehouses before being sent on to Babylon, which would
thus control the international market. What a boom there would
have been in antiquity! The mastery of the caravan routes had
always been the primary concern of Mesopotamian rulers and
the source of war on many occasions. But the project, though by no
means an impossible undertaking, never materialized. The desert
sun, the tracks which led nowhere, the deadly fevers poisoning
the bloodstream, the torments of thirst, the solitudes of unknown

[65]

[63–66] Assyrian reliefs depicting the military exploits of the rulers and the overthrow of their enemies. (*British Museum.*)

[64]

[65]

] The Central Palace at Nimrud: Campaigns of Tiglath-Pileser III. Archers in action,
iege tower, and, top left, the impaled prisoners. Eighth century B.C. (*British Museum.*)

[68] Minister to the King of Assyria, from the Palace at Khorsabad. (*Louvre.*)

[69] Slaves on heavy transport duties, from the Palace of Sargon at Khorsabad; eighth century B.C. (*Louvre*.)

[70] Assyrian horseman: seventh century
B.C. (*Louvre.*)

72] Assyrian ships transporting timber: relief from the Palace of Sargon at Khorsabad. Eighth century B.C. (*Louvre.*)

71] Royal Attendants, from the Palace of Sargon at Khorsabad, eighth century B.C. *Louvre.*)

[73] Winged genius carved on the walls of an Assyrian Palace. (*Louvre.*)

[74] Prisoner of war carrying child. (*Louvre.*)

[76] Gilgamesh, the hero of the Creation Epic: from the Palace of Sargon at Khorsabad. Eighth century B.C. (*Louvre.*)

[75] Human-headed bull guarding the entrance-way to the Palace of Sargon at Khorsabad. Eighth century B.C. (*Louvre.*)

[78] Fine Assyrian head. End of eighth century B.C. (*Louvre.*)

[79] Figure of Assyrian: relief from the Palace of Sargon at Khorsabad. Eighth century B.C. (*Louvre.*)

[77] Servant before the royal chariot: relief from the Palace of Sargon at Khorsabad. Eighth century B.C. (*Louvre.*)

[80] Slaves bearing the war-chariot of the Assyrian King: relief from the Palace of Sargon at Khorsabad. Eighth century B.C. (*Louvre.*)

erritory—these were afflictions hard enough to bear on the march in war; but the soldier had always the hope of victory, or ts actual achievement, to spur him on, and the fruits of battle provided no mean compensation for his hardships. To reconnoitre n the desert on a hazardous commercial enterprise, with nothing out sand for booty, was a totally different matter, a rash expendi-ure of human life and equipment for a goal that existed only in the mind of the king.

But it was largely due to the vision and determination of Nebuchadnezzar that, for a time at least, the metropolis of Babylon became the principal thoroughfare for the commerce of India, and, which was even more of an achievement, he ruined the commercial influence of the Phoenician merchants in Arabia. This success moreover encouraged him to lose no time in attacking Tyre, the Carthage of Western Asia and the old mercantile rival of the empires of Mesopotamia.

The destruction of Tyre was clearly prophesied by Ezekiel: 'Therefore thus saith the Lord God; Behold, I am against thee, O Tyrus, and will cause many nations to come up against thee. . . .

'I will bring upon Tyrus Nebuchadnezzar King of Babylon, a king of kings, from the north, with horses, and with chariots, and with horsemen, and companies, and much people. . . .

'And he shall set engines of war against thy walls, and with his axes he shall break down thy towers. . . .

'And I will make thee like the top of a rock: thou shalt be a place to spread nets upon.'

The citadel of Tyre stood high upon an island, heavily defended. It held out against Nebuchadnezzar for no less than thirteen years. When the Phoenicians eventually submitted a heavy tribute had to be paid, but Nebuchadnezzar did not achieve the final destruction of this stubborn city. The end was to come some centuries later at the hand of Alexander the Great; Tyre was replaced by Alexandria.

A fragment of a religious text indicates that Nebuchadnezzar invaded Egypt in the thirty-seventh year of his reign. Although we have no historical record from the Babylonians to confirm this, it is more than likely that Nebuchadnezzar planned such an in-vasion, which according to Biblical tradition sounded a knell of doom for the empire of Pharaoh. The Hebrew prophets saw in this the hand of Jehovah fulfilling the promise made of old to smite with the sword the rulers of the Nile Valley, and they ex-horted their people to prepare for the hour of deliverance. The

B.—D

story is told of the founding by Nebuchadnezzar of 'Babylon in Egypt', near Memphis, to ensure that he was not forgotten in the valley of the Nile.

The political success of Babylon certainly gained her complete supremacy over her weak and moribund neighbours. These were the finest days of all her lengthy history. The Age of Nebuchadnezzar may be compared with the Age of Augustus or that of Louis XIV. The capital became the bank of the ancient Orient; she was virtually unassailable and enjoyed a time of prosperity that was without precedent in her annals. Nebuchadnezzar was worshipped by his people as if he were a god. Parents called their male children Nabu-kur-usur-ilu which means 'Nebuchadnezzar is God', or Nabukudur-usur-Shamshi, 'Nebuchadnezzar is my sun', or again Nabuch-abni, 'Nebuchadnezzar is my creator'.

They were a fortunate people. War, to them, was a highly lucrative business. It was possible to avoid conscription by paying a tax or contributing towards the maintenance of a soldier; they had no use for military service. What mattered to them, so far as the king's victories were concerned, was not the glory of battle so much as the fact that it was a means of consolidating their economic supremacy. Armies had to be maintained for the sake of trade; they needed feeding, but it was not necessary to pay them well. The Babylonians were fond of good living; there was nothing particularly heroic about them. Apart from the merchants and small traders, quite a large section of the population must have been absorbed in one way or another by the various religious activities. Rites and ceremonies and festivals, some of which were lengthy and complex, were taking place almost continuously and required the services of large numbers of priests and priestesses, musicians and chanters of incantations, and secular assistants of all kinds.

To give thanks to the king for the benefits he had bestowed on them, and to show him their appreciation, the people erected in his honour a statue of solid gold weighing over four tons. This monumental effigy was erected on a hill to the south of Babylon; it dominated the Mesopotamian plains and glittered in the dazzling rays of the sun, huge and fantastic, the blazing token of a glory as short-lived as life itself. Endless processions came to bow down before the golden monster. Nebuchadnezzar's achievements had turned the city into an international centre for every kind of commercial and religious activity. Like an octopus Babylon extended her tentacles around her, quietly and methodically. On the

northern route the moving ribbon of her caravans stretched towards Ecbatana, capital of the Medes; from there, slipping east-
wards by way of the Caspian Gates, it reached Alexandria of Asia
(Herat). Here the caravans diverged, on the one hand towards
Bactria and on the other in the direction of India by way of
Arachosia, whence three new trading routes were opened up. There
was a route to the Mediterranean, first running north along the
Euphrates and then slanting off to the west, branching into
innumerable tracks which traversed Phoenicia, Palestine, and the
land of Moab (now Jordan), and reached Pelusium in the Egyptian
Delta. Finally there was a pack trail that led from India to Babylo-
nia, whence the Indian products were exported to Persia, Cilicia,
Phrygia and Lydia, terminating at Sardis. Small wonder that
Babylon was prosperous. Nebuchadnezzar might well believe that
his work would last forever. Inscriptions everywhere, engraved
high up in the rock, spread wide his glory. The texts of the Wadi
Brisa and of the Nahr el Kelb near Beirut all tell how the monarch
sent to cut down the cedars of Lebanon for the construction of the
Temple of Marduk and Nabu at Babylon.

Having achieved an omnipotence seldom paralleled in history,
Nebuchadnezzar cherished the customary desire for a long and
prosperous life. The dominant idea expressed in the glyptic of this
period, on the cylinders and royal seals, is prayer: a priest, his hand
raised to his lips, stands before the divine emblems, usually those
of Marduk and Nabu, which are shown on an altar. To persuade
the gods to look with favour upon his empire and defend the line of
succession forever, Nebuchadnezzar dedicated fifty-four temples in
their honour, and restored and developed the city 'for the dwelling-
place of his sovereignty'. The monarch enumerates certain works
which he undertook at great expense to embellish his capital:

'When the god Marduk, the great Lord, created me, he commanded me solemnly to maintain order in the land, to raise cities,
to rebuild the temples. I obeyed, full of fear. I established Babylon,
the sublime city . . . and her great walls, the Imgur-Enlil and
the Nimid-Enlil. On the threshold of her gates I set huge bulls
and footed serpents, such as no other king before me had wrought.
My father had surrounded the city with walling in asphalt and
burnt bricks; for my part I established a further mighty wall
alongside the others, and united it with the walls of my father. I
laid their foundations on the very threshold of the netherworld, and
raised them up mountain high. My father had built beside the
Euphrates a quay in burnt bricks, but he did not complete it. I, his

first-born, the favourite of his heart, established the Arakhtu wall in asphalt and burnt bricks, and fortified the wall built by my father. Esagila, that fearful sanctuary, the great house of heaven and earth, the dwelling-place of the gods; Kaduglisug, the dwelling-place of the goddess Zarpanitum; Ezida, the dwelling-place of the king of heaven and earth; these I made to shine like the day. I rebuilt Etemenanki, the *ziggurat* of Babylon. At Borsippa I rebuilt the lofty temple, the temple beloved by Nabu; with a covering of gold and precious stones I made it resplendent like the firmament.'

We are never likely to know what happened to Nebuchadnezzar during the last years of his adventurous reign. He shut himself up in a kind of mysticism, seeking the company of the wandering shades of the netherworld, the kingdom of Nergal. His soul became filled with terror, and he consulted the most learned of his divinators; he crouched in a spiritual darkness like a beast at bay, crying aloud in his solitude at the flames which seared his body, the demons which tore him apart. He spent his days in an agony of mind, believing that he, Nebuchadnezzar the Great, was possessed by the devil at the will of Marduk. Had he offended the gods to be sunk so low, more wretched than the meanest of his subjects? The people of Babylon began to be alarmed at the strange silence of their king, who no longer took any part in public affairs. A rumour began to get about, first in whispers, then more blatantly; the gossip of palace officials reached the ears of the world outside, and soon the whole of Babylon was buzzing with the news. 'Marduk has forsaken Nebuchadnezzar! Marduk is deserting Babylon and her people!'

Panic swept over the populace. A hostile crowd gathered in front of the palace, besieging it in ever growing numbers, restive, clamouring and lamenting, refusing to accept betrayal by their gods. Why should the whole city suffer because the king was out of his mind? Let him be thrown to the dogs, but Babylon and her people who love Marduk must be spared affliction. Let Nebuchadnezzar show his face to his assembled people, let him appear in the midst of them, he who was once their gracious benefactor. Let them pay homage as before, rich and poor alike, before their king so long beloved. . . .

But the people of Babylon waited in vain, gripped by a terrible fear. 'Nebuchadnezzar has sinned! He has provoked the wrath of Marduk! The fury of the gods is upon us all. Let him expiate his sin, let him make honourable amends! The gods do not wait for a sinner to die before redressing a wrong by punishment.' But Nebuchadnezzar was hemmed in by the seven evil ones which gnawed at his body while he slept. He was molested by demons deriding him, by the evil of his own soul, and he hid himself away from the eyes of his people, shutting his mind to the tumult outside. A sickly anguish was devouring him like a worm inside a fruit.

He summoned his priests, divinators, and astrologers, only to chase them away like dogs. Let them return to their smoking entrails, their boxes of perfumes, their infinite universe of planets, if he, whose glory was to shine for all eternity, was denied that peace of mind he sought so bitterly. He hurled invective at the gods, and dragged himself on his knees before them. Around him everything, even the shadows, were deformed into menacing creatures lit up by the flames of hallucination. He before whom the world had trembled had become a travesty of his former self. Bowing his face to the earth, he entreated the gods to forgive him his sins, humiliating himself before them: 'Lord, my sins are many and my transgressions are grave. . . . God is vexed with me. May he be appeased! May he deliver my afflicted body from all its pain and distress. May he deliver my tormented heart! May he deliver my soul!'

After forty-two years of triumphant achievement the reign of Nebuchadnezzar, and with it the hegemony of Babylon, was approaching the end. Legend has it that the ageing Nebuchadnezzar had a presentiment of what would come to pass. In a lucid interval, seized with prophetic fever, he gathered together his officials, priests, royal functionaries, followers and slaves. From the lofty terraces of his palace he showed them the city below, and his words rang out: 'I, Nebuchadnezzar, prophesy unto you the misfortune which will befall, which neither Marduk, my Creator, nor Sin, nor Ishtar, have succeeded in persuading the goddesses of destiny to turn aside. A Persian mule will come, with his own gods to assist him. He will impose servitude upon you. His accomplice will be a Mede, whom Assyria once honoured. Would to the gods that before betraying his fellow citizens he had perished by drowning, in a whirlpool or in the sea, or wandered in the desert where there are neither cities nor paths trodden underfoot by man, and where the wild beasts roam at will, to be lost in the barren rocks of the ravines.'

This 'Persian mule' of whom the old king spoke was Cyrus the Achaemenian, who, clapping thrice with his hands, was to bring about the fall of Babylon. The king's life slowly ebbed away. The sepulchre was made ready; evil spirits hovered everywhere, hideous and expectant. For the last time Nebuchadnezzar was attired in all his noble battle array, and in death he 'shone as if amidst the heavens'. And following the funeral cortège of that prodigious king came Nabonidus the Pious, destined to be the last of the Royal House of Babylon.

And the Jews, remembering Jerusalem in the depths of their Babylonian ghettos, took up their tambourines and chanted a new song of deliverance: 'Set ye up a standard in the land, blow the trumpet among the nations, prepare the nations against her. . . . For out of the north there cometh up a nation against her which shall make her land desolate. . . .'

The last years of Nebuchadnezzar darkened a brilliant reign, one of the greatest in the history of the world. He too might have recorded upon stone, as did Assurbanipal before him, the poignant reflections of a great man who, at the summit of his achievements, suddenly senses a deep futility: 'Since . . . I have done good to god and man, to the dead and the living, why is it that disease, heartache, distress and destruction are clinging to me? Distress of soul, distress of body have bowed my form. I spend my days sighing and lamenting. . . . Death is making an end of me. . . .'

Nebuchadnezzar did not escape the power of the demons of the Babylonian world, those ruthless portents of evil which were not to be ignored. Too many fantasies had brought about a premature old age. How many conquerors, whose exploits have become so exaggerated in the course of time that they have come to lose the flavour of reality, have felt that in the long run their victories after all were of no account, and have come to know at the end of their days, as he did, a bitter melancholy burning its way like an acid into the soul. The words of an older writer might have been those of Nebuchadnezzar:'My strength is running out; I see a bad fate. My tomb is open and my dwelling-place is taken possession of before I am dead. Misfortune is at my heels. . . .'

Astute administration and inspiring leadership had characterized both Hammurabi and Nebuchadnezzar and produced a rich response in the people of Babylonia. But there is little evidence of either in the years that followed the death of Nebuchadnezzar. It would have required no lack of determination and vigour to deal effectively with the political complications besetting Mesopotamia at this turning-point in her history; and since no less than three successive kings are recorded in the next eight years it is hardly surprising that the tide began to turn against Babylon. The advent of Nabonidus, who may have been installed by the priesthood in the hope of nobler achievements in the name of the gods, brought no improve ments in her fortunes. His interests lay in peaceful pursuits, in building and restoration, religious activities, and the study of ancient records. And it was to Belshazzar his son that he preferred to delegate the business of politics and the defence of the Empire.

Meanwhile, a new power had come into being to the east of Mesopotamia. Persia, under Cyrus the Achaemenian, was to show that a policy of expansion could be achieved without wholesale destruction. His strength had already proved greater than that of the Medes, whose kingdom he had united with his own, establishing his capital at Ecbatana. Victorious also in Asia Minor and on his eastern frontiers, Cyrus turned his attention to Babylon, the control of which would bring him the mastery of Syria and the western coast. Marduk himself, the god of Babylon, had, according to Cyrus, directed his footsteps towards the city, 'going as a friend by his side'.

It is difficult to disentangle fact from fiction in the various accounts of the fall of Babylon in 539 B.C. Cyrus states quite simply that Marduk allowed him to enter the city 'without a struggle or combat'. A contemporary inscription records that 'the whole of the people of Babylon, the whole of Sumer and Akkad, the great men and the governors of the cities bowed under him, kissed his feet, were delighted with his sovereignty, their faces glowed'. It would be surprising if the Babylonian welcome were quite so cordial, and if there was little resistance it is likely that the city was taken completely by surprise. The fortifications of Babylon, thanks to the work of Nebuchadnezzar and his predecessors, were almost impregnable, and the city's resources were such that the Babylonians had no reason to fear a prolonged siege. The entry of Cyrus, according to Herodotus and Xenophon, was effected by means of a daring piece of strategy. The River Euphrates, which flowed through the city, was diverted by the Persians into a great trench constructed outside the walls, so that the army, on a night when the people of Babylon were engaged in a religious festival, was able to advance into the city along the dry river-bed. And in the words of Xenophon: 'Owing to the vast size of the place, the inhabitants of the central parts, long after the outer portions of the town were taken, knew nothing of what had chanced, but . . . continued dancing and revelling until they learnt the capture but too certainly.'

The independence of Babylon was ended forever. But Cyrus, who regarded the taking of the city as the liberation of the Babylonian people, conformed from the first to their traditional practices, and legitimized his succession as king of Babylon by 'taking the hand of the god Bel'. And before twelve months had passed he ordered the release of the Jews from captivity. Their gold and silver vessels were restored to them, and in 537 B.C. they departed, over forty thousand in number, to rebuild their temple at Jerusalem: 'Then they shall know that I am the Lord their God, which caused them to be led into captivity among the heathen: but I have gathered them unto their own land, and have left none of them any more there.'

The Achaemenian Empire under Cyrus established three great capitals, at Susa, Ecbatana, and Babylon. By the time of Darius, the ninth ruler in the Persian succession, the Empire had become 'the most extensive in the history of the world', and included Mesopotamia, Syria, Egypt, Asia Minor, the Greek cities and islands, and part of India. From these ancient civilizations, with their wealth of tradition and genius and their abundance of material resources, came the finest artists and craftsmen of the time to serve the Persian king. A text of Darius, who lived for a time at Babylon, commemorates the building of his magnificent palace at Susa, designed and decorated in the Babylonian style with lions, bulls, and mythological creatures in coloured enamelled bricks: ' . . . This is the palace which I built at Susa. From afar its ornamentation was brought. Downward the earth was dug, until I reached rock in the earth. When the excavation had been made, then rubble was packed down, one part 40 cubits in depth, another (part) 20 cubits in depth. On that rubble the palace was constructed.

'And that the earth was dug downward, and that the rubble was packed down, and that the sundried brick was moulded, the Babylonian people, it did (these tasks). The cedar timber, this—a mountain by name Lebanon—from there it was brought; the Assyrian people, it brought it to Babylon; from Babylon the Carians and the Ionians brought it to Susa. The *yaka* timber was brought from Gandara and from Carmania. The gold was brought from Sardis and from Bactria, which here was wrought. The precious stone lapis-lazuli and carnelian which was wrought here, this was brought from Sogdiana. The precious stone turquoise, this was brought from Chorasmia, which was wrought here. The silver and the ebony were brought from Egypt. The ornamentation with which the wall was adorned, that from Ionia was brought. The ivory which was wrought here, was brought from Ethiopia and from Sind and from Arachosia. The stone columns which were here wrought—a village by name *Abiradus*, in Elam—from there were brought. The stone cutters who wrought the stone, these were

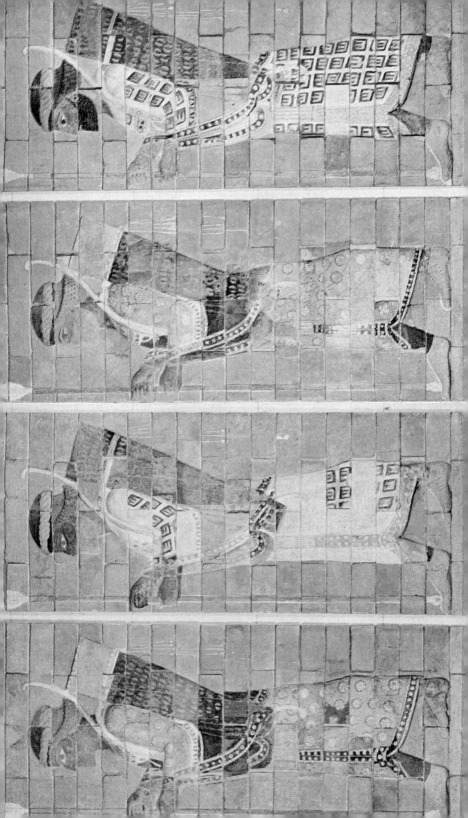

Susa: The Palace of Artaxerxes II. Frieze depicting the royal Achaemenian archers.

(Fourth century B.C. *Louvre*)

Ionians and Sardians. The goldsmiths who wrought the gold, those were Medes and Egyptians. The men who wrought the wood, those were Sardians and Egyptians. The men who wrought the baked brick, those were Babylonians. The men who adorned the wall, those were Medes and Egyptians. Saith Darius the King: At Susa a very excellent (work) was ordered; a very excellent (work) was (brought to completion). Me may Ahuramazda protect, and Hystaspes, my father, and my country.'

The famous palace of Darius at Persepolis, built shortly afterwards, was in many respects similar to that at Susa and was the work of the same craftsmen. Here, on the terrace, his successor Xerxes erected a huge structure flanked by winged human-headed bulls resembling those that guarded the palace entrances of the Assyrian rulers. And in his great 'hall of a hundred columns', unfinished at the time of his death, the king was represented in bas-relief in the form of a hero triumphing over monsters, a favourite theme in Babylonian art recalling the ancient Sumerian Epic of Gilgamesh.

The Achaemenian Empire of Persia was destined to last for another two hundred years after the fall of Babylon, though its influence gradually declined towards the end. With the rise of Alexander the Great it was finally overthrown; and in the course of his last campaigns the Macedonian entered Babylon, where he was hailed as a deliverer. The Persian governor was retained in accordance with the usual policy of Alexander, but he gave orders to rebuild the great temples destroyed by Xerxes. The restoration of the staged tower of Babylon appears however to have been an impossible undertaking; 'It was thought that ten thousand men would not be able to remove the fallen rubbish in two months. Alexander planned a great rebirth of the city as a maritime trading centre linking India and Egypt. But on his return to Babylon in 323 B.C., in the course of preparing a new campaign in Arabia, he developed a fever and died. And with his death, Babylon was abandoned.

* * *

Of the art of the Babylonians we have relatively few examples in the two major destructions of the city, first by the Hittites and later by Sennacherib, much of the treasure of Babylon was lost From Assyria there is far more material, particularly in the form of bas-reliefs and sculpture, many examples of which can be studied in the Louvre or the British Museum. In touching briefly on this

complex subject it is only possible to outline certain features which
may be said to characterize Mesopotamian art as a whole, and
which are not as a rule to be found in the works of art familiar to
us in Western Europe.

Mesopotamian art might be described as highly conventional.
To our eyes it appears unemotional, a simple statement of the
nobler aspects of life or the disasters of war. Time and again in the
bas-reliefs the defeated, dead or suppliant, are depicted lying on
the ground, their eyes already fixed on the netherworld. The
characterization and attitudes, their line, height and movement,
were established once and for all on a set pattern, remaining the
same century after century. The figures carved on the historical
reliefs adorning the palaces had to be stereotyped according to the
relative importance of their social status. One must remember that
the craftsman was faced with the task of conveying some activity
not once but a thousand times over, according to the prescribed
rules; thus the formal portrayal of scenes from life had to be free of
such complexities as volume or dimensions. Bold incision was what
really mattered to give life and light to the granite of the stele or
walling.

The Babylonians and Assyrians, like many of their predecessors,
seem to have been unaware of aesthetic pleasure such as we might
derive from a particular shape or delicate colouring. The Assyrians
were not great painters, apart from their platters and goblets, and
only two colours appear to have been used, as is indicated by the
cakes of colouring matter found in the outbuildings of the palace
of Sargon at Khorsabad: one a red which is sesquioxide of iron, and
the other a blue made from pulverized lapis-lazuli which the
craftsmen applied with a sticky coating on bricks of dried clay
covered with lime. The whole idea of perspective, and the use of
blurred outline and nuance, were foreign to the Mesopotamian
artist. 'His approach was intellectual. For him the elements com-
posing a scene were treated entirely according to their relative
importance: the higher the rank, the greater in size; a god had to
be bigger than a king; a king had to be bigger than a queen; and
the royal subjects had to be correspondingly smaller. Moreover,
while we take account of proportion and the rules of perspective in
laying out the diverse elements of a scene, oriental art will often
portray a scene as if from some imaginary central viewpoint. The
four sides of the horizon are laid out flat like the four sides of a box.
But the commonest practice is that of the Amarna school: the
spectator is supposed to be standing directly in front of the scene

represented, and although the relative proportions are observed there is no foreshortening, because the notion of perspective does not arise.' (*Le Paysage dans l'Art de la Mesopotamie ancienne,* by M. Rutten, *Syria,* 1941).

The material on which the artist had to work obviously did not lend itself to subtlety of approach. The impact of his art is rather like a blow on a gong, resounding and triumphant, without any of the softening effect of minor variations, which can induce a receptive state of mind by suggesting or emphasizing the nature of the figures portrayed or the meaning of an object. A series of symbols was employed: a leaf sufficed to represent the luxuriant vegetation of the Mesopotamian palmgroves. 'Distant features of landscape appear as if in the foreground, either superimposed as it were in mid-air, or distributed between different levels, from top to bottom or vice versa according to where the main action of the relief is taking place.' The artists depicted, not what they saw, but what they knew to be the case. They rarely show a three-quarter view, since the actual dimensions of the object had to be adequately represented. Landscapes are rare and lack fluidity of line and local colour. Water is represented by undulating lines, oceans by loops, hills by scallops; the earth is a striped lozenge, and so on. The animals on the later vases are often geometric, and the principal figures become silhouettes engraved only in outline.

But Mesopotamian art, such as it is, presents an invaluable historical record, and we can hardly ask more of it than that which it was officially intended to convey. It was designed to recount on the walls of temples and palaces the triumphant exploits of the kings and the gods, in monumental friezes which were meant to be informative rather than appealing to the eye. Ordinary everyday life with its pleasures and pastimes was not portrayed. It was an official art, with magical and religious significance, not an art to be savoured by the élite for its aesthetic merit, but one which might well have been employed, perhaps intentionally, for propaganda purposes. Such art would not have required the services of an interpreter to convey in a flash to the world outside what it meant to be a great and formidable empire.

IV

THE CITY OF BABYLON

IN the Akkadian story of the Creation, Babylon was built 'in the beginning of time' by the lesser celestial deities, as a dwelling-place for the great gods. When the work was completed there was great rejoicing, and Marduk, Creator and Lord of Heaven and Earth, addressed the assembled gods: 'This is Babylon, the place that is your home; Make merry in its precincts, occupy its broad (places).'

The site of Babylon was certainly occupied in prehistoric times, as is attested by flint implements and other stone objects recovered there. The Sumerian name for it was *Ka-Dingir-Ra*, which became in Akkadian *bab-ili*, or *Bab-ilani*, 'gate of the god' or 'gate of the gods'. A temple referred to as E-sagila and associated with the worship of Marduk appears to have existed at Babylon from early times; it was rebuilt and endowed by Sargon of Agade and later destroyed during the Sumerian revival under the Third Dynasty of Ur. Babylon, before it became a great political capital in the eighteenth century B.C., had been an ancient religious centre, and retained this function throughout the city's history.

In 1898 the eminent archaeologist Robert Koldewey was entrusted by Kaiser Wilhelm II and the German Oriental Society with the task of carrying out a systematic excavation of the site of Babylon. The work went on for eighteen years, and many distinguished specialists took part in it, including B. Meissner, Lindl, F. Weissbach, W. Andrae, J. Jordan, A. Nöldeke, G. Buddensieg, O. Reuther, F. Wetzel, F. Baumgarten, F. Langenegger, J. Grossmann and K. Müller. The size and complexity of the site made its investigation a vast undertaking. Excavations in the residential quarter known as Merkes, the oldest part of Babylon, disclosed a series of occupation layers, the most recent being Parthian, a few feet below the surface. Farther down were the Hellenistic, Persian and Neo-Babylonian levels; and lower still, those of the Assyrians and the Kassites. At forty feet down lay the ruins dating to the time of Hammurabi and the First Dynasty of Babylon. Below these it was impossible to investigate because of the rise in the water level.

The archaeological evidence, therefore, does not take us further
back in the history of the city than about 1800 B.C. And although
Koldewey was able to form an approximate idea of the plan of the
houses and streets in the Merkes area from the time of the Kassites
onwards, he had only somewhat fragmentary evidence from other
parts of the site of building prior to the Neo-Babylonian era. For it
must be remembered that the city was virtually obliterated at the
hand of Sennacherib. Most of the remains revealed by excavation
can be identified as the work of Nebuchadnezzar. But Koldewey's
work has shown that in general outline Babylon preserved the
same essential features throughout her history; the plan of the city
remained relatively unchanged from the time of Hammurabi to
that of Cyrus.

When Herodotus visited the city of Babylon in the fifth century
B.C. he recorded many interesting details that had been preserved
since the Neo-Babylonian period: 'The city is divided into two
portions by the river which runs through the midst of it. This
river is the Euphrates, a broad, deep-swift stream, which rises in
Armenia, and empties itself into the Erythraean Sea. The city wall
is brought down on both sides to the edge of the stream: thence
from the corners of the wall, there is carried along each bank of the
river a fence of burnt bricks. The houses are mostly three and four
storeys high; the streets all run in straight lines, not only those
parallel to the river, but also the cross streets which lead down to the
water-side. At the river end of these cross streets are low gates in
the fence that skirts the stream, which are, like the great gates in
the outer wall, of brass, and open on the water. The outer wall is
the main defence of the city. There is, however, a second inner
wall, of less thickness than the first, but very little inferior to it in
strength. The centre of each division of the town was occupied by
a fortress. In the one stood the palace of the kings, surrounded by a
wall of great strength and size: in the other was the sacred precinct
of Jupiter Belus, a square enclosure two furlongs each way, with
gates of solid brass; which was also remaining in my time. In the
middle of the precinct there was a tower of solid masonry . . .
upon which was raised a second tower, and on that a third, and so
on up to eight. The ascent to the top is on the outside, by a path
which winds round all the towers. When one is about half-way up
one finds a resting-place and seats, where persons are wont to sit
some time on their way to the summit. On the topmost tower there
is a spacious temple, and inside the temple stands a couch of unusual
size, richly adorned, with a golden table by its side. . . . They also

declare—but I for my part do not credit it—that the god comes down in person into this chamber, and sleeps upon the couch.'

—The staged tower here described by Herodotus was the Biblical Tower of Babel: 'And it came to pass, as they journeyed from the east, that they found a plain in the land of Shinar; and they dwelt there. And they said one to another, Go to, let us make brick, and burn them throughly. And they had brick for stone, and slime (bitumen) had they for mortar. And they said, Go to, let us build us a city and a tower, whose top may reach unto heaven. . . .' To the Babylonians the tower was known as Etemenanki, 'House of the foundation of heaven and earth'; it was the most famous of all the *ziggurats* of ancient Mesopotamia, dating in all probability from the third millennium B.C. and many times restored. What Herodotus refers to as 'solid masonry' was in fact a huge construction of mud-brick, with layers of reed matting inserted at intervals to afford drainage as well as extra strength. The tower became a ruin at the hands of Xerxes before the rest of the city fell into decay, but its fame was such that many later travellers exploring the neighbourhood described in fanciful detail the phenomenal 'Tower of Babel' they were convinced they had seen. Not far from Baghdad the ruins of the red *ziggurat* of Aqarquf, like a huge heraldic sign, still rise to a height of 187 feet above the level of the plain, and right up to the end of the eighteenth century this tower was commonly mistaken for that of Babylon. The confusion of mounds and ruins in the locality, and the equally confused legends that were attached to them, are evident from the narrative of John Cartwright, who visited Baghdad and the neighbouring area in 1603: 'Two places of great antiquity did wee throughly view in the Countrey; the one was, the ruins of the old Tower of Babel (as the inhabitants hold unto this day) built by Nimrod, the Nephew of Cham, Noah's Sonne. And now at this day, that which remayneth is called the remnant of the Tower of Babel; there standing as much as is a quarter of a mile in compass, as high as the stone-worke of Paul's Steeple in London. It was built of burnt Bricke, cimented and joyned with bituminous mortar, to the end, that it should not receive any cleft in the same. The Brickes are three-quarters of a yard in length, and a quarter in thicknesse, and betweene every course of Brickes there lieth a course of Mats made of Canes and Palme-tree leaves, so fresh, as if they had been layd within one yeere.

'The other place remarkable is the ruines of old Babylon, because it was the first citie which was built after the Floud. Some doe thinke that the ruines of Nimrod's tower, is but the foundation of this Temple of Bell, and that therefore many Travellers have beene deceived who suppose that they have seene a part of that tower which Nimrod builded. But who can tell whether it be one or the other? It may be, that confused chaos which wee saw was the ruins of both, the Temple of Bel being founded on that of Nimrod.' (*Purchas his Pilgrimes*, Vol. VIII, pp. 520 ff.)

The 'Temple of Bell', or 'Bel', is presumably that which Herodotus called 'the sacred precinct of Jupiter-Belus'. The god Bel, which meant 'Lord', was Marduk, whose temple Esagila, associated with the founding of Babylon, stood close to the *ziggurat*. The temple and tower, though separate constructions, together symbolized Babylon, home of the gods and centre of worship, around whose precincts grew up the great capital city bearing the same name.

The outer city wall built by Nebuchadnezzar was a double construction crowned with look-out towers, and had a circuit of just over eleven miles. A remarkable feature was its magnificent causeway along the top. This was large enough to allow a chariot along it with a team of four horses abreast, and even for two chariots to pass each other quite easily. This aerial avenue was, like the 'Hanging Gardens', one of the wonders of the ancient world, and one can imagine that the Babylonian chariots, 'swift as the wind', must have been an impressive sight aloft upon such a fantastic highway. There was also an inner encircling wall, again a double fortification, extending along both banks of the Euphrates. This construction was of unburnt brick, and its two component walls were known as the Imgur-Enlil and the Nimid-Enlil. Their building and restoration are chiefly associated with the work of Assurbanipal, Nabopolassar, Nebuchadnezzar and Nabonidus.

Nebuchadnezzar records the completion of his outer defensive system with evident satisfaction: 'That no assault should reach Imgur-Enlil, the wall of Babylon; I did, what no earlier king had done, . . . at a distance so that it (the assault) did not come nigh, I caused a mighty wall to be built on the east side of Babylon. I dug out its moat and I built a scarp with bitumen and bricks. A mighty wall I built on its edge, mountain high. Its broad gateways I set within it and fixed in them double doors of cedar wood overlaid with copper. In order that the enemy who devised (?) evil should not press on the flanks of Babylon, I surrounded it with mighty floods, as is the land with the wave-tossed sea.'

[81] Desert warfare. (*British Museum.*)

[82] Men bringing offerings: relief from the Palace of Sargon at Khorsabad. Eigh
century B.C. (*Louvre*.)

[83] Contest with daggers: relief from the Palace of Sennacherib at Kuyunjik (Nineveh). The participants' are depicted in human form with grotesque animal heads and legs that terminate in the powerful talons of a bird of prey. Eighth-seventh century B.C. (*British Museum.*) DEMONS

[84] Capture of Susa by Sennacherib. The city is shown in the top register, with its name in cuneiform characters. It is deserted, the population having gone forth to submit to the Assyrians. In the middle register women and children follow a band of musicians; in the lowest the corpses of men and horses and the debris of their equipment are borne away by the river Kerkha. Seventh century B.C. (*British Museum*.)

[85] Plumed horse with groom:
detail from an Assyrian frieze.
(*Louvre.*)

[86] Assyrian priest wearing divine winged apparel. In a small container he carries a mixture of oil, butter, and honey used in anointing. (*Louvre.*)

of Sennacherib at Nineveh. Seventh century B.C. (British Museum.)

[88] Detail from a frieze at Nineveh depicting captives taken in war. Seventh century B.C. (*Louvre*.)

[89] Assurbanipal, represented carrying a builder's basket, as the restorer of
Esagila, Temple of Marduk at Babylon. Seventh century B.C. (*British Museum.*)

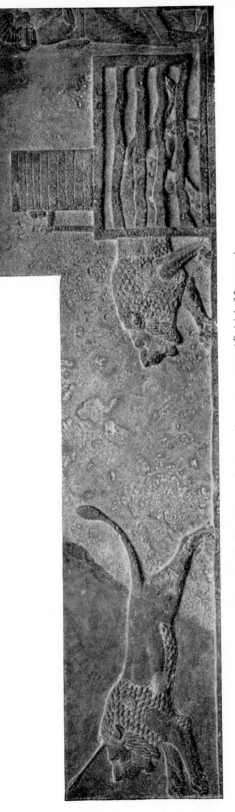

[90] Detail from the Lion Frieze of Assurbanipal at Nineveh: seventh century B.C. (*British Museum.*)

[91] Assurbanipal: Ceremonial Rite. The king is attended by fan-bearers and a bowman, and is pouring a holy libation on four slain lions. He stands before an altar beside which is the *marru*, triangular symbol of Marduk. The ceremony is carried out to the accompaniment of the harp. The inscription begins: 'I am Assurbanipal, King of Assyria. In my abounding princely strength I seized a lion of the desert by his tail . . .'. (*British Museum.*)

(a)

(b)

[92] Two examples of North Syrian art from the first millennium B.C. (*Louvre.*)

(a) Stele of Neirab.

(b) Stele from Marash: the woman with the child and a bird.

[93] Clay tablet from South Babylonia, seventh century B.C. This shows an outline map of the regions of the world, and bears an inscription relating to the conquests of Sargon of Agade, who reigned towards the end of the third millennium B.C. (*British Museum.*)

[94] Sippar: Tablet of King Nabu-apalidinna. The tablet commemorates the king's restoration of the temple of Shamash, the Sun-god. Above the head of Shamash are the symbols of the moon, sun, and the planet Venus, and the Sun disc is on the altar. The shrine rests upon the Celestial Ocean, which is indicated by wavy lines.

This scene is rendered in the archaic style, the costumes and other features resembling those of the third millennium B.C. Seventh century B.C. (*British Museum.*)

[95] Babylonian horned dragon, symbol of the
god Marduk: in bronze. Sixth century B.C. (*Louvre.*)

[96] Figure of Ninhursag, goddess of childbirth: from
the sanctuary of Shushinak at Susa. (*Louvre.*)

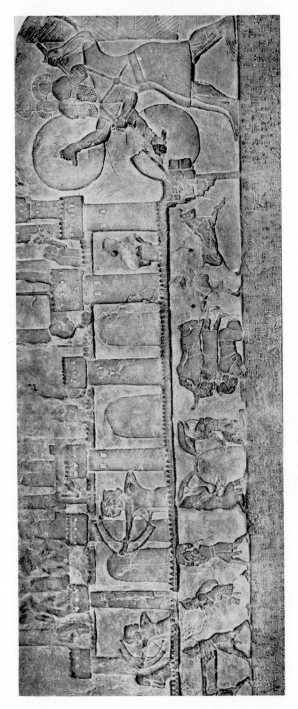

[97] Destruction of a Babylonian city. (*British Museum.*)

The eight city gates were dedicated to the principal deities worshipped by the Babylonians. Perhaps the most famous of all was the Gate of Ishtar, which was on the north side of the city. To the east was the Gate of Marduk, and also that of Ninurta, god of hunting and of war; and to the south, the Gate of Urash, an old Akkadian deity of the holy city of Dilbat not far south of Babylon. These four gates were all found and excavated by Koldewey. In addition he was able to identify the sites of four more with reasonable certainty: to the north, the Gate of Sin, the Moon God; to the south, the Gates of Enlil, the Sky God, and Shamash, the Sun God; and to the west the Gate of Adad, the Storm God.

The track from the north was the best and most frequented. The traveller arriving by this route would make his way through the palmgroves and across the fields, past sundry habitations on the outskirts of the city, where the streets would be alive with tradesmen and loafers, men on horseback, carts and chariots. Not far from the inner wall of the city he would come to the magnificent Processional Way, which would lead him up through the Gate of Ishtar and eventually to Esagila, the Temple of Marduk, and the towering *ziggurat* Etemenanki. This avenue, which extended for the best part of a mile, was one of the most beautiful in the ancient world, the Champs Elysées of Babylon, bordered with temples and palaces. On the east side, just past the Ishtar Gate, stood the Temple of Ninmah, goddess of the dead; it was flanked with towers, and characteristically decorated, as a sacred building, with vertical grooves. Koldewey found it in a fairly good state of preservation, with its cella, postament, priests' apartments and store-rooms all recognizable.

A little farther on was the Temple of Ishtar of Agade, constructed on the usual plan, with a well for water in the courtyard, and the altar outside, facing the entrance to the temple. In the cella Koldewey found a foundation casket made of brick and containing a small carved figure. This shrine, like most of the monuments of Babylon, was many times restored, particularly by Nebuchadnezzar. It stood in the residential quarter known as Merkes, the oldest part of the town, with its alleyways paved with flagstones, its small gardens and courtyards with deep wells, its cubic houses, flat-topped and windowless, strange surrealist buildings, stark under the noonday sun and mysterious at dusk. It was in this quarter that Koldewey found, beneath the foundations of the bigger private houses with their solid walls of unburnt brick, and considerably below the Neo-Babylonian level, tablets dating to the First Dynasty

of Babylon. These tablets were lying undisturbed in a thick layer
of ash from a fire that ravaged the city some thirty-five centuries
ago.

/ Herodotus noted that the streets of the great city were for the
most part straight, a familiar feature of many modern American
cities. In this portion of the city there are no open spaces suggestive
of markets or public squares, and it appears to have been a somewhat congested quarter, though clearly planned on systematic lines.

On the other side of the Processional Way, a little farther back,
lay the Southern Citadel, a vast complex of buildings which included the Palace of Nebuchadnezzar, and whose construction took
many decades and a prodigious amount of forced labour to complete.
The Citadel must have been visible a long way off; it was high up,
between the Euphrates on the west, the Processional Way on the
east, the inner city wall on the north, and the canal Libilhegalla on
the south. The Palace of Nebuchadnezzar was built as a monu-
ment to the genius and might of the kings of Babylon: 'Because my
heart did not wish the dwelling-place of my Majesty to be in
another place, because I did not build a royal dwelling in any other
place . . . my dwelling-place in Babylon grew insufficient for the
dignity of my Majesty. Because the fear of Marduk my lord dwelt
in my heart, I did not change his street in order to widen my
fortress, the seat of my royalty in Babylon. I did his sanctuary no
damage, nor did I dam up his canal, but I sought at a distance
room for myself. I made . . . a lofty seat for my royal dwelling of
asphalt and burnt brick, and joined it to the palace of my father.
In a not unfavourable month, on a propitious day, I grounded the
foundations firmly on the bosom of the underworld, and raised its
summit high like mountains. . . . I caused mighty cedars, the
product of high mountains, . . . and selected fine cypresses to be
laid lengthwise for its roofing. Door leaves of *mismakanna*, cedar,
cypress, and *usû*-wood and ivory inlaid with silver and gold and
adorned with copper; bronze hinges and thresholds I fitted into its
doorways, and caused its summits to be encompassed with a blue
cornice.'

The main entrance lay through the Gate of Beltis, guarded, as
were all the Palace entries, by basalt lions like those of the Assyrian
palaces. This led directly into the eastern court, the first of the five
great courts of the palace, and doubtless a scene of ceaseless activity
on the part of the royal servants, guards, scribes, and *bârû*, all
going about their business in the immense royal citadel. These
spacious open courts, whose gateways were adorned with brightly-

coloured lion friezes in enamelled brick, led to the Throne Room, scene of the famous feast of Belshazzar. Grouped round the various courtyards, and accessible by means of alleyways and passages, were the quarters reserved for the garrison, the domestic and administrative offices, the king's private apartments, and the harem. Koldewey thought that a royal flagon ware was made on the premises, for he found in the course of his excavations here a large number of elegantly-shaped vases known to the Greeks as alabastra.

Much of the official business was conducted in the palace court-yards; the taxpayer lamenting his pecuniary difficulties before the official assessor must have been a familiar spectacle. Certainly not even the most practised magician with a whole battery of amulets could have made the sharp-witted tax-collectors or their all too flattering assessments vanish into thin air! War trophies from distant lands adorned these open courts. One might find a stele of the Hittite god Teshup, bearer of the North Wind; statues from Mari, the ancient rival of Babylon; bas-reliefs blackened by fire and stolen from Nineveh; stelae of the ferocious Assurbanipal of Assyria; or that famous basalt Lion of Babylon, which may be of Hittite origin, trampling a man to death.

To the south of the Palace lay the Throne Room of the Babylo-nian Kings, an immense apartment measuring roughly fifty-six yards by nineteen. This was the Holy of Holies of temporal sovereignty, just as Esagila was that of the almighty and universal god Marduk. It was a magnificent chamber, with its long façade brilliantly enamelled. The decoration, against a blue ground, con-sisted of garlands of palmettes and columns topped by double capitals, enamelled in gold, black, white, yellow and red, and enhanced by the brightly coloured frieze of lions on the gateway to the court. The total effect must have been remarkably cool and refreshing in contrast to the burning blues of the Mesopotamian sky.

The palace was particularly celebrated amongst the historians of antiquity as the site of the 'Hanging Gardens of Babylon'. It is thought that the gardens were built by the king to remind Amyitis, daughter of the King of the Medes, who became his wife for diplomatic reasons, of the trees and flowers of her native land. This wonder of the ancient world has been a constant source of specula-tion. It was presumably visible from a long way off, and was the crowning grace of Babylon. Some of the oldest legends, still extant, attribute this aerial garden to the work of Semiramis, that enig-matic, amorous queen of Assyria. According to classical writers,

people came from far and wide to see this tranquil island of green
suspended between heaven and earth above the roofs of Babylon.

Not much is known for certain about the Hanging Gardens, but
there is an interesting tablet recently deciphered by Contenau
from which it appears that there was a certain Babylonian king
named Marduk-apal-iddin who took a passionate interest in botany
and *planted in the Garden* certain varieties of plants, for culinary
and medicinal purposes. A scribe drew up the catalogue of these
species and his text ends with the words: 'Plants of the Garden of
King Marduk-apal-iddin of Babylon . . . whosoever reveres
Marduk, may he not remove the tablet of the King.'

It is also known that Koldewey uncovered what he took to be the
probable foundations of the famous edifice, in the north-east angle
of the palace near the monumental blue Gate of Ishtar, just north
of the first palace courtyard. He also found the well from which
water was raised to the upper levels. This ingenious device with
buckets would have made it possible to keep the garden plantations
regularly watered in all stages of the building, which rested on a
solid vaulted construction comprising fourteen rooms. This formidable stone structure, measuring 47 yards by 33, was itself surrounded by walling built to absorb any movement of the subsoil by
a series of expansion joints. As Koldewey points out, stone was a
most unusual building material to find in Babylon, and the construction was obviously planned with the utmost care.

The foundation of the colossal causeway known as the Processional Way was made up of many layers of bricks covered by a
layer of bitumen. Large flagstones of fine limestone and red
breccia formed the pavement, every slab bearing the same inscription: 'Nebuchadnezzar, King of Babylon, son of Nabopolassar
King of Babylon, am I. The Babil Street I paved with blocks of
shadu stone for the procession of the great Lord Marduk. Marduk
Lord, grant eternal life.' Another inscribed brick, slightly more
informative, also refers to the construction of this street: 'Nebuchadnezzar, King of Babylon, he who made Esagila and Ezida glorious
son of Nabopolassar, King of Babylon. The streets of Babylon, the
Procession Streets of Nabu (god of writing and destiny) and Marduk
my Lords, which Nabopolassar, King of Babylon, the father who
begat me, had made a road glistening with asphalt and burnt
bricks: I, the wise suppliant who fears their lordship, placed above
the bitumen and burnt bricks a mighty superstructure of shining
dust, made them strong within with bitumen and burnt bricks as a
high-lying road. Nabu and Marduk, when you traverse these

streets in joy, may benefits for me rest upon your lips; life for
distant days and well-being for the body . . . May I attain eternal
age!' Another interesting find by Koldewey in one section of the
roadway was that of a few bricks inscribed with the name of
Sennacherib. This bloodthirsty Assyrian had been sufficiently well-
disposed towards Babylon to enhance the city at some stage in his
reign, afterwards sacking it utterly in a fit of rage.

The decoration of the Processional Way was the work of Nebuchadnezzar. On each side of the avenue, for a distance of just over
200 yards, ran a magnificent enamelled frieze. It displayed a series
of lions modelled in bas-relief—sixty on each side—brilliantly
coloured and standing out at regular intervals against a plain
background of light or dark blue. Some of the figures were
enamelled in white with yellow manes, some in yellow with red
manes, the latter now green owing to decomposition. These
intractable monsters must have been a terrifying sight, open-
jawed, with flairing nostrils and threatening fangs, their claws out—
a fine welcome for the stranger entering Babylon, leading as they
did to the serpent-headed dragons and enormous bulls on the Gate of
Ishtar. Foreigners, bringers of tribute, traders and potential enemies
alike were not likely to forget that first tremendous impression of
Babylon, unlike anything they had ever seen before. The permanent
presence of these savage beasts as the guardians of the city was no
doubt reassuring to the Babylonians, and served as a solemn warning
to intending assailants that for them this Processional Way which
led to the heart of the city could prove a Highway of Death.

This majestic approach to Babylon was entirely in keeping with
the noble splendour of the Gate of Ishtar, through which the
traveller entered the city. This too was one of the finest constructions of Babylon, and the inhabitants were proud of it. Its walls
were ornamented with thirteen rows, superimposed, of brick
reliefs in brilliant enamels, dragons alternating with bulls,
arranged in such a way that they seemed to be advancing to meet
the approaching stranger. The ruins still stood to a height of 40 feet
at the time of the excavation. Koldewey noted the ingenuity of
the Babylonian builders in constructing this gateway and elsewhere
on the site. To prevent the foundations of the structure from crack-
ing, they had devised the expansion joint, a precaution still used in
the case of walls that are not built in one piece, but adjoin each
other, the foundation of one being shallower than the other. The
idea is to leave the two parts of the wall standing free of each other;
a narrow vertical space is left between them from top to bottom.

As an additional safeguard, lest any slight movement in the sub-soil should tilt the walls out of the perpendicular, the Babylonians sometimes joined on a vertical fillet to the wall with the shallower foundation, and this slid in a groove in the main wall. Koldewey also discovered that in the case of certain small isolated foundations the substructure of burnt brick was laid on a bed of unburnt bricks shaped like a well and filled up with loose earth; thus it could 'shift about at the base without leaning over, giving it play like the joints of a telescope'.

It has been calculated that there were at least 575 reliefs of bulls and dragons adorning the Gate of Ishtar, and their effect must have been staggering. Here again we find the signature of Nebuchad-nezzar: 'Both entrances of the town gate had become too low owing to the filling up of the street of Babil. I dug out that town gate, I grounded its foundations facing the water strong with bitu-men and baked bricks, and caused it to be finely set forth with baked bricks of blue enamel, on which wild oxen and dragons were pictured. I caused mighty cedars to be laid lengthwise for its ceiling. Door leaves of cedar covered with copper, threshold and hinges of bronze I fitted into its gates. . . . The same town gateways I caused to be made glorious for the amazement of all peoples.'

The lion was the favourite animal of Ishtar and a decorative motif utilized in Babylonian art at all periods. We have already seen that it adorned the Processional Way. But the bull was commonly the symbol of Adad, god of divination, of the lifegiving rain and the devastating hurricane. His statues were often decorated at the base with a pair of walking bulls; his emblem, the thunderbolt, is sometimes placed upon the back of a recumbent bull. Similar representations indicate that the dragon, or *sirrush*, was the sacred animal of Marduk and of his son Nabu, god of the neighbouring town of Borsippa, he who inspired the epic, patron of scribes, and bearer of the tablet of destiny.

Dragons such as those that appear on the Ishtar Gate are to be seen on many of the boundary stones and official seals. They were renowned in the ancient world, and tally with the description to be found in the story of Bel and the Dragon from the Apocrypha. It is also possible, as Koldewey suggests, that the high priest of Esagila, seeking to attest in realistic fashion the presence of the god in the temple, kept an arval or other local species of reptile, to be exhibited on festival days in the half-light of the sanctuary. At the sight of a living dragon on this sacred spot the hearts of the faithful wor-shippers would indeed have been filled with terror and awe.

In artistic conception this *sirrush* is quite unlike other fabulous
beasts which exist in great numbers in Babylonian symbolism. It is
less fantastic than the gigantic winged bulls with human heads of
the Assyrian palaces, or the crowned and bearded men with the
body of a bird and the tail of a scorpion. The dominant feature of
the *sirrush*, as Koldewey has pointed out, is his scaly coat, with the
long serpent-like tail. Behind his head are two spiral crests resembling those of a Chinese dragon; the tail ends in a small curved sting;
the forelegs are those of a rampant feline, while the hind ones are
those of a bird of prey, covered with scales and armed with powerful
talons. In addition to his scales, this fabulous creature possesses hair.
Now, *these are the characteristic features of the prehistoric dinosaur*.
By what mystery is it that we find, adorning the monumental
Gates of Ishtar at Babylon in the sixth century B.C., a representation
of a monster which disappeared before the Flood, when immense
salt lakes covered Western Asia from the foothills of the Lebanon
to the central plateau of Persia, from the confines of Arabia to the
mountains of Armenia now shining with glaciers and icefields?
Here is a problem for which as yet there is no answer. . . .

Ishtar was the great goddess of love and death. She was identified
with the planet Venus, and was the goddess of the evening and of
the morning. Her father was the moon-god, Sin, her brother the
sun-god, Shamash:

'Fulfilling that which is ordained by my father, Sin,
I rise, I rise in perfection;
'Fulfilling that which is ordained by my brother, Shamash,
I rise, I rise in perfection.'
Fervent prayers were addressed to her for help and deliverance:
'I pray to thee, O Lady of ladies, goddess of goddesses
. . . O gleaming one, Ishtar, assembler of the host
. . . Where thou dost look, one who is dead lives;
One who is sick rises up; the erring one who sees thy face goes
    aright.
I have cried to thee, suffering, wearied, and distressed, as thy
    servant.
. . . Faithfully look upon me and hear my supplication.
Promise my forgiveness and let thy spirit be appeased.
Pity! for my wretched body which is full of confusion and trouble.
Pity! for my sickened heart which is full of tears and suffering.
. . . Loosen my fetters; secure my deliverance. . . .'

But at the sound of the trumpets of war Ishtar was hailed by every citizen-in-arms as the Lady of Battles, fearless and savage against her enemies. She incited the people to insurrection and sedition. The soldiers, drunk with her presence, acclaimed her when she appeared amongst them in the height of battle; for it meant that Ishtar looked with favour upon the blood-drenched earth and the mounting heaps of the slain. They would kill, and perish gladly, blinded by her glory.

Ishtar was also a fertility goddess, through whom alone the pleasures of love could be achieved. She fell in love with the hero Gilgamesh, according to the ancient Epic: 'Come, Gilgamesh, be thou my lover! Do but grant me of thy fruit. Thou shalt be my husband and I will be thy wife. I will harness for thee a chariot of lapis and gold. . . . . Humbled before thee shall be kings, lords, and princes!'

But Gilgamesh would have none of her. She made a journey to the Netherworld, where, before each of the seven gates of the 'Land of No Return', she was stripped bit by bit of her ornaments and clothing. Her sister, who was Queen of the Netherworld, was suspicious of her intentions, and had her imprisoned in the shadows of Nergal, letting loose upon her the sixty miseries. On earth, meanwhile, these adventures were having disastrous effects, all fertility and reproduction having ceased in the absence of the goddess. Her brother Shamash became uneasy for the future of the world, and he eventually succeeded in rescuing Ishtar before it was too late.

There are many legends of kings risen from obscurity who came to the throne through the love of Ishtar. It was she who allotted to each the length of his reign and bestowed upon him the throne and royal insignia. At Babylon she was the bright star of heaven and earth. She had her gate, her sacred way, her district, her temples; the Temple of Ishtar of Agade already mentioned was a small sanctuary with a special function, possibly associated with her aspect as the morning star, but there were probably several others. One, built for Ishtar of Babylon, in the thirteenth year of the reign of Apil-Sin of the First Dynasty of Babylon, was enlarged, embellished, and faithfully maintained by various later kings and continued in existence until 94 B.C.

But her worship and her sacred temples were by no means confined to a single Mesopotamian city. Ishtar, the 'Lady of Pleasures', incorporated in one deity all the goddesses of Sumer, Akkad, Assyria and Babylonia. In another part of the prayer already quoted, the worshipper asks:

Lion guarding the Temple of Dagan at Mari.

(Bronze. Early second millennium B.C. *Louvre*)

'Where is not thy name, where is not thy divine power?
Where are thy likenesses not fashioned, where are thy shrines
   not founded?
Where art thou not great, where art thou not exalted?'

She was the comforter of kings who sought her alliance, even of
Assurbanipal whose heart was cruel: 'The goddess Ishtar heard my
anxious sighs, and, "Fear not!" she said, and filled my heart with
confidence. "Inasmuch as you have lifted your hands in prayer
(and) your eyes are filled with tears, I have mercy".' She was
regarded as the great Mother, and one of her oldest effigies is that
of a woman pressing her breasts between her hands to make the
milk gush forth. Figures of Ishtar have been found on numerous
sites and have been thought to bear a close resemblance to certain
prehistoric figurines, some of which go back to the Stone Age of the
Near East and Mediterranean area. She is also, as is written in the
Revelation of St. John: 'the woman clothed with the sun, and the
moon under her feet, and upon her head a crown of twelve stars'.
On the Assyrian stele of Til Barsib she is portrayed with the
symbolic eight-pointed star enclosed within a circle; she carries
two quivers crossed on her back, and on the left side she wears
a sword; she stands on a lion and her right hand is raised in a gesture
of benediction.

Goddess of love and goddess of death—Ishtar of Babylon was the
symbol for human passions in all their aspects of good and evil. Her
temples were rich and numerous and her perfumed *ishtaritu* fer-
vently dedicated themselves to her service. She was the paramount
incarnation of feminine power, and through it of fecundity. New
peoples gave her new names, but by them all she was honoured as
'the most august of all goddesses':

'Praise the goddess, the most awesome of the goddesses.
Let one revere the mistress of the peoples, the greatest of the
   Igigi. (Celestial gods.)
Praise Ishtar, the most awesome of the goddesses.
Let one revere the queen of women, the greatest of the Igigi.
She is clothed with pleasure and love.
She is laden with vitality, charm, and voluptuousness.
In lips she is sweet; life is in her mouth.
At her appearance rejoicing becomes full.
She is glorious; veils are thrown over her head.
Her figure is beautiful; her eyes are brilliant.
The goddess—with her there is counsel.

The fate of everything she holds in her hand.
At her glance there is created joy,
Power, magnificence, the protecting deity and guardian spirit.
She dwells in, she pays heed to compassion and friendliness.
Besides, agreeableness she truly possesses.
Be it slave, unattached girl, or mother, she preserves (her).
One calls on her; among women one names her name.
. . . .
She is sought after amongst the gods; extraordinary is her station.
Respected is her word; it is supreme over them.
She is their queen; they continually cause her commands to be
    executed.
All of them bow down before her.
They receive her light before her.
Women and men indeed revere her.'

The festivals given in her honour brought each year to Babylon
an influx of nomads and foreigners eager to participate in the
general rejoicing, the drinking orgies and the consummatory rites.
Strabo gives a disapproving account of what went on in the city
during these great feasts. The pleasures of the flesh clearly played
an important part in the veneration of Ishtar the hermaphrodite.
But whatever the licentiousness of the back streets and alleyways,
this was a highly religious festival. Ishtar, in the shadow of her
temple, presided over the dedicatory rituals peculiar to her cult.
Votive maidens chanted their prayers before her: 'I praise thee and
beseech thee, Sovereign Queen, Almighty Goddess, O Thou most
fair, who dost inflame me with desire, Protector of armies, inscrutable Goddess of men and women.' Her votaries lived and dwelt in
the temple, lovely and alluring in their delicate veiling. But they
were not alone in their earnest wish to serve the goddess. To the
holy precincts of the shrine there came the men who also sought to
give themselves in complete humility to her service forever by the
rite of self-castration, carried out before the inscrutable presence
of the deity.

Outside, in a swarming and tumultuous Babylon, the festival
would be in full swing. Every now and again an officiant from the
rites would come to the river's edge to throw in a sheep's head
fresh from a sacrifice. In the temple precincts, servants would be
setting up their cooking pots, and offerings in the form of joints of
meat, entrails, and juices of various kinds would be brought for the
gods, the king, the priests and their hopeful families, the goldsmiths, silversmiths and weavers. The teeming inhabitants of the

city would be soaking themselves in spiced wine, mead, and beer
and stuffing themselves with kidneys, cucumbers, and palm-hearts
Servants all over the city would be preparing the symbolic torches
scented with aromatics, and all night long there would be an in-
describable din of music and merry-making, shouting and singing
In the glow of thousands of braziers lit in the houses and in the
streets and squares, the people of Babylon would offer up banquets
to the gods and to the wandering spectres of the dead who are
eternally in need of sustenance.

At such a feast, which would go on for days on end, a stranger to
the city might well become bemused in no time by the constant
hubbub and the attentions of amulet sellers, herbalists, and provo-
cative courtesans. Pushed and shoved by the clamouring crowd—
—there were a million inhabitants—and having perhaps had a drop
too much of that excellent palm wine from the Damascus region,
continuously on guard against mischievous devils and all the hover-
ing parasites that swarmed disguised to tempt the gullible; beset by
traffickers in perfumes and drugs and all the lure of the poppy-seed;
dazed by colour and splendour everywhere, the visitor to Babylon
would be swept into a prodigious throng, gathered respectfully
before a motley display of mysteries: divinators, casters of spells,
bird-watchers, bone-setters, astrologers with their carefully regu-
lated tables of conduct, and the ubiquitous tellers of dreams. Freud
would indeed have been in his element here, where every dream
was immediately subjected to expert scrutiny, classification, and
interpretation. . . .

One might picture another ceremony in honour of Ishtar. It
would have taken place in the evening, as soon as the first stars
appeared, sparkling over the boundless plains. The city would be
hushed. A virgin, hitherto secluded in the quiet of the temple,
would be led forth by the *urigallu*, custodian of the holy place, who
knew the Creation Epic inside out and could repeat the litanies in
Sumerian before the divine image. With him would come the
Initiates, along with the magicians and chanters of spells, and the
procession would move slowly off towards the *ziggurat* of Babylon.
Exorcists in their red robes would escort the maiden, driving away
to left and right the male and female demons that were always
trying to coil themselves up in the human soul and entrails. There
would be servants in attendance carrying the sacred Torch, which,
once it had lit the braziers of the temples, houses, streets and gates
of Babylon, could not be extinguished except with milk from a
camel. Chanters would be singing their prayers in the form of

psalms, accompanying themselves on kettle-drums made with ox-skin, and dulcimers popularly known amongst the urchins of Merkes as 'Ladies' tongues'. Eunuchs would be playing airs on the flute to which they danced as they went along, to charm away the spirits which floated like luminous circles in the spacious night. . . . And, before the multitude which had assembled to watch the age-old rites, the votive maiden of Ishtar would slowly climb the seven-staged way to the top of the *ziggurat*. There she would enter the sanctuary of Marduk, to remain throughout the night to await the visitation of the god. The crowd which watched might well be stricken with a holy awe. She who was chaste had seemed to enter into the very sky, her body an offering, the living offering of her people to their national god, the mysterious spouse of a night with no tomorrow; a night which for her would be eternity. . . .

From the great Gate of Ishtar, past palaces and temples and private houses, stretched the sacred Processional Way of Babylon. This long and stately avenue at length turned west, to lead to holy ground: on the left, to the sanctuary Esagila, Temple of Marduk the Creator, without whom there would be no life on earth; and on the right, to Etemenanki, the lofty *ziggurat*.

Esagila, 'the House with the Lofty Head', was one of the finest constructions of Babylon, dazzling the eye with its lofty cupola covered in gold leaf. The date of its foundation is unknown. A foundation cylinder found by Koldewey in the course of his excavations attests the restoration of Esagila by Assurbanipal: 'Under my government the great lord Marduk held his entry into Babil with rejoicing and entered upon his dwelling in Esagila forever. The regular offerings of Esagila and of the gods of Babylon I established, the protectorship of Babil I retained. . . . I filled Esagila with silver and gold and precious stones, and made Ekua shining as the constellations in the sky.'

Nebuchadnezzar, the 'fosterer of Esagila', as he called himself in his inscriptions on innumerable bricks, also contributed to the embellishment of this sanctuary: 'Silver, gold, costly precious stones, bronze, *mismakannu*, and cedar wood, all conceivable valuables . . . the product of the mountains, the wealth of the sea, a heavy burden, a sumptuous gift, I brought to my city of Babil before him, and deposited in Esagila, the palace of his lordship, a gigantic abundance. Ekua, the chamber of Marduk, I made to gleam like the sun. Its walls I clothed with solid gold instead of clay or chalk, with lapis and alabaster the temple area. Kahilisir, or the "door of state", as also the Ezida gate of Esagila, I caused to be made bright as the sun. Du-azag, the place of the naming of destiny . . . the chamber of the lordship of the wise one among the gods, the exalted Marduk, that an earlier king had furnished with silver, I clothed with shining gold, a magnificent adornment . . . like unto the stars of heaven. . . . My heart impels me to build Esagila, I keep it perpetually before mine eyes. The best of my cedars, that I brought from Lebanon, the noble forest, I sought out for the roofing over of Ekua, the chamber of his lordship, with deliberate care, the mightiest cedars I covered with gleaming gold. . . . For the restoration of Esagila I make supplication every morning to the king of the gods, the lord of lords.'

Marduk had so distinguished himself in the course of the early struggles of the Creation that he was accorded, by a unanimous decision of the gods, the kingship of heaven and complete sovereignty over the universe which he had made. His abode was Babylon, which thus became, in Hammurabi's words, 'supreme in the world', its fortunes eternally linked with the destiny of the city's national god. His temple was the serene embodiment of the soul of a noble city that led the world; and to the people of Babylon it must have seemed the symbol of a civilization that could never be destroyed without the downfall of the entire universe which Marduk had created.

Amongst all the many gods brought back from time to time in the course of campaigns and raids into foreign lands, Marduk remained supreme, the life-spring of Babylon. The historical records of the Hammurabi period already attested his greatness and his appeal to the heart and spirit of the Babylonian people, and the scribes wrote down his commands upon the tablets: 'When Marduk commissioned me (Hammurabi) to guide the people aright, to direct the land, I established law and justice . . . thereby promoting the welfare of the people.'

Only the Jews and their prophets, in the centuries to come, were to dare to defy the great god of Babylon and predict the fearful desolation that was to be. The rich Amorite city was untroubled by such prophecies; her people were protected by a god who was dominant in all his aspects. He was Nergal, god of the spectres of hell; Nabu, god of writing; Sin, who illuminated the night; Shamash, god of the sun, whose rays were eternal; and Adad, god of rain. He was the pivot of the Wheel in its eternal rotation. His presence was an unfailing strength against the invisible evil ones that hovered everywhere. He endowed his followers with good fortune and sustenance, and bathed the spirits of the dead in his

heavenly light. Assurbanipal bowed down before him: 'In the first
year of my reign, when Marduk, king of the universe, put into my
hands the rule of Assyria, I laid hold of the hem of the garment of
his great godhead, I gave my attention to his sanctuaries.' He was
'the firmament which shines in the sky', through whom everything
came into being and passed away:

'Marduk is able to revive in the grave.
Zarpanit (his consort) knows how to deliver from destruction.
Wherever the earth reaches, the heavens are spread out,
The sun shines, fire glows,
Water flows, the wind blows,
(Wherever the beings) whose clay the goddess Aruru has nipped off,
Creatures endowed with breath, stride rapidly,
. . . as many as there are, glorify Marduk!'

A representation of Marduk found on a cylinder of lapis-lazuli from
Babylon, dating to the ninth century B.C., has been described in detail
by Edouard Dhorme: 'The god wears a tall cylindrical headdress,
which is plumed and ornamented with rosettes. He is bearded, and
his hair is dressed behind his head in curls. A long robe sprinkled
with encircled stars falls to his feet. In his left hand, which is raised
in front of him, he holds the insignia of power: the sceptre and
diadem. In his right he grasps the *harpesh* (a kind of ritual weapon
resembling a scimitar). Marduk is guarded by the *mushrushshu* or
'red snake'' (the *sirrush*), whose likeness is represented on the
enamelled bricks of the Gate of Ishtar at Babylon; it has a horned
head, scaly body, tail of a scorpion, forefeet of a lion, and hind legs with
the talons of a vulture. This creature is a survival of the winged
dragons which decorate the libation vase of Gudea. The forces of
the animal kingdom—quadruped, bird, fish, and reptile—are here
concentrated into one individual in the service of the god, to assist
in the struggle against evil powers.'

It was to Esagila of Babylon that all the great soldiers and illustrious princes came to seek the divine blessing, the consecration of
their glory and crowning of their achievements. The lofty crene-
lated walls of the temple surrounded a reserved quarter of the city
which was a world of its own, administered from within. Around
the immense sanctuary were grouped the official quarters for the
priests, functionaries, servants, interpreters of oracles, and divinators. There were gardens, cattlesheds, stables, workshops, and the
kennels of the sacred dogs belonging to the deity; cellars and store-
rooms and the chambers of chattering hairdressers who attended

the divine consort Zarpanitum. The precincts were sacred; no one, under pain of impalement before one of the eight gates of Babylon, was permitted to disturb the devotions of the priests who served the illustrious god of the people. At once a palace, a place of rejoicing, and a stronghold, the 'House with the Lofty Head' had to protect the deity from violation and guard the riches lovingly heaped up in its secret rooms. Esagila had been built in order to 'rejoice the heart' of its divine guest, who had come to dwell in the midst of humanity solely to shield and magnify the fruit of his labours.

'It seems to have been the general custom', writes Charles-F. Jean, 'from earliest times, both in Assyria and Babylonia, to honour the national god with a festival, whose central rite was the processional march of the god from his temple or principal place of the city to a sort of temple of pleasure some distance away: the name *akîtu* was given both to the special sanctuary and to the festival itself.' This was the Festival of the New Year at Babylon and was the occasion for tremendous scenes of fervour and rejoicing, everyone taking part in immense processions joined by delegates from far and wide. In Babylon the *akîtu* of Marduk began the New Year in the month of Nisan. The public ceremonies went on for twelve days. On the seventh day, which was observed with the most solemnity, it was the most splendid of all the processions which made its way from the temple Esagila to the *akîtu*. An Akkadian tablet gives the complete text of the ceremonies which took place when the gods came forth to their *akîtu*. The document is particularly illuminating in relation to the functions of the *urigallu*-priest, who was in charge of the daily procedure, the opening of the doors of the temple, the ritual prayers, and the delegating of purifying and sacrificial rites. In the course of his duties he had to recite the Creation Epic twice from beginning to end, a task of some magnitude. The king had to go through a rite of penitence before the *urigallu*, who absolved him and promised the divine blessing: 'He shall strike the king's cheek. If . . . the tears flow, the god Bel is friendly; if no tears appear, the god Bel is angry: the enemy will rise up and bring about his downfall.' This symbolic ritual appears to have been part of a re-enactment of the death and resurrection of Marduk in order to promote by magical means the regeneration of the crops; the New Year Festival was essentially a fertility rite, which had to be strictly observed in every detail; and it was moreover essential for every king of Babylon to participate in this ceremony and to 'take the hand of the god Bel' before his enthronement could be considered complete. The great procession must have been

[8] The pleasant city of Deir es Zor on the Euphrates. The waterfront of Babylon may
ve looked very similar.

[99] A convoy halts on the river-bank.

[100] The Euphrates crossing is made by *kelek*, a type of skin-raft known to the Assyrians.

[101] Nomads in the main street of Hassetshe. For them the town is full of attractions.

[102] Tribesman with sword.

[103] Ahmed, a friendly purveyor of sherbet.

[104] On the banks of the Jaghjagha, near Tell Hamidi, the women are filling their water-skins.

[105] Hassetshe: The sheikh goes about his business.

[106] The Bedouins have a liking for long tresses and eye cosmetics.

[107] Milk from the goat and camel provides most of the nomad's daily sustenance.

[108] On a warm afternoon one feels all the better for a short nap.

[109] Pullet for sale: what offers?

[10] Deir es Zor: the old quarter of the city. At Babylon in the Merkes quarter the
ouses were very similar.

[111] A village in Upper Mesopotamia at noon. In such shade as there is, the
thermometer would register 106°F.

[112] Near Nisibin in the Jebel Sinjar region. In the shadow of the tent the tribal poet evokes the glories of the past.

[113] Sunset on the Euphrates, at Deir es Zor.

ne of considerable splendour and brilliance, as the gods came forth
n their chariots in their finest array, with their ceremonial weapons
nd distinctive emblems, to the sound of chanting and incantations.
The period of this festival marked a time of rebirth throughout the
arth, and its final days were given up to time-honoured festivities
n the worship of nature.

—Of all the lofty monuments of Babylon the towering *ziggurat*
must certainly have been one of the most spectacular constructions
f its time, rising majestically above its huge encircling wall of a
housand towers. It was famed throughout the ancient world and
drew a host of travellers of every race and creed to worship and
admire. Etemenanki, 'House of the foundation of heaven and
arth', stood high above the city, commanding the river valley rich
with palms, the central structure of a huge enclosure measuring
oughly 500 yards square. Twelve monumental gateways gave
ccess to this great court, no doubt guarded in the traditional
manner by gigantic animal figures of repellent aspect.

Around the vast square chambers were set aside for pilgrims, as
well as for the priests who looked after the *ziggurat*, and Koldewey
alled this collection of buildings the 'Vatican of Babylon'. The
priests of Etemenanki must have held positions of high rank as temporal representatives of the king of the gods, from whom the rulers of
Babylon derived their sovereignty and who shielded the city against
assault. Their private dwellings were large and luxurious and it is
easonable to assume that the enclosure of Etemenanki was the
hief administrative centre for the various high priests and officials.
Here, in the secret inner chambers, one might expect to find the
acred cult objects, gold, silver and precious stones, the chariots of
Marduk and other deities, the processional barks brought out on
estival days, musical instruments used in the rites, solar emblems,
and couches and thrones of gold.

Built by a remarkable race of men to defy the passage of time,
Etemenanki seems to have conveyed a sense of unequivocal
greatness to the ancient world. Yet for all its great fame we know
ittle about it. Apart from a tablet recording its dimensions,
he observations of Herodotus, and the little that Koldewey
was able to glean in the course of his work on the site, we
have practically no reliable information as to its appearance, and the
exact purpose it served is still largely conjectural. Today, as Parrot
ecords, 'where once there stood what was perhaps the most
gigantic structure of Babylonian civilization, there is an enormous
hole, full of water. . . .' Koldewey himself reported that the

destruction to the *ziggurat* was 'irreparable', vast quantities of material having been quarried away for building purposes.

From the evidence of the tablet, which dates to 229 B.C., but is thought to be a copy of an older text, Parrot concludes that Etemenanki, 'on a base 295 feet square, rose with its seven storeys to a height of 295 feet', and he thinks that a temple stood on top. Herodotus mentions eight towers, with a temple in or on the topmost tower. Koldewey was unable to distinguish more than the ground plan, from which it was impossible to tell how many stages there were to the tower. But *ziggurats* at other Mesopotamian sites have been better preserved; from earliest times it became customary to build temples on raised platforms, and these terraced structures came to be built up in stages, one on top of another, as time went on. There have been many theories to explain the function of the *ziggurat*, but it is generally agreed that it was a religious structure of some kind. Strabo thought that the purpose of Etemenanki was to provide a resting-place upon its summit for the tomb of Marduk, where it would be close to heaven, out of reach and inviolable. Others have taken the view that these staged towers were built by priests to assist them in their astronomical observations.

Thousands of tablets preserved in the temple archives record the astronomical observations of the Babylonians over many centuries. They learnt the use of the sun-dial and the water-clock in calculating in advance the movements of celestial bodies in relation to each other, and invented the 'luni-solar' calendar as a reliable method of measuring time. This consisted of twelve months of thirty days each, with an intercalary month inserted at regular intervals. The application of their mathematical genius brought many practical benefits in everyday life; but it sprang from a religious belief that influenced their every activity.

For these observers, whose knowledge was deeply rooted in primitive ideas, the heavenly bodies which they studied over the centuries were living gods, whose ordered movements in space, correctly interpreted, could be used as a guide in the daily activities of men. Astronomy, for the Babylonians, began as a means whereby the astrologer was enabled to advise on public or private issues, on the pursuit of peace or war, or on the sale of a patch of land. But there was more to this than the purely utilitarian angle. One can discern an underlying vast philosophical system, in which man was eternally linked with the movements of the celestial bodies, whose laws were immutable and inescapable. All life was but an infinitesimal part of the universe. The gates of knowledge had been opened

Mesopotamia: Palace of Mari. Part of a sacrificial scene, restored by Paul François, architect to the expedition of M. André Parrot, from thousands of tiny fragments.

(Wall painting. Early second millennium B.C. *Louvre*)

by these ancient men of learning, who from the lofty *ziggurat* had
received the revelation of the march of time. The future was
boundless. They perceived a relation between the mathematical
units in terms of which the sensory world could be expressed, and
the vast creative force divinely revealed in the eternal cycle of death
and resurrection. Behind the mystery of cyphers and sacred num
bers they had long discerned the 'spiral' of the universe and of the
gods.

The orientation of Etemenanki to the four cardinal points of the
compass had been ritually observed in terms of sacred numbers.
The building was thus in the eyes of the ancient peoples much more
than a symbol; it represented the exact centre of space, from which
the supreme vital force radiated out over the whole earth, attesting
the presence of their Creator Marduk.

And so the kings of Babylon sought to enhance this sacred edifice.
Nabopolassar received from Marduk the order to restore the
ziggurat, 'to lay its foundations firm on the bosom of the under
world, while its top should stretch heavenwards'. Before beginning
the task, before touching a single brick of Etemenanki, he con
sulted the oracles in the course of a sacrificial feast to discover which
day would be propitious; then: 'For Marduk, my lord, I bowed my
neck, I undid the raiment which clothed my Majesty, I trans
ported bricks and clay upon my head.' Before this picture of the
pious monarch as it appears in later Babylonian texts, the customary
image of a haughty omnipotent ruler fades out for a moment. But
the king was carrying out a ritual transmitted from one generation
to the next. On the 'Day of Reconstruction' he duly went forth
accompanied by his priests, his musicians and chanters of laments,
divinators whose task it was to invoke the five gods of magic, and
poets to utter the ritual words, to stand before Etemenanki.

The first task was to seek out and bring to light, with the help of
a special axe sanctified by the High Priest, the *temenu*, which was
the Sumerian name for the foundation text, usually engraved on a
small cylinder or votive nail. These nails, in bronze or clay, with
the head of a god, had the power to drive off evil spirits from their
hiding-places. The king then anointed the *temenu* with honey,
cream, beer and oil, and re-laid it, taking care to conceal its position.
The rites had to be strictly observed; if any detail were overlooked in
the preliminaries to reconstructing a building, the offender was put
under a curse. Before laying down the bed of bricks which would
constitute the foundation of the new structure, it was essential to be
absolutely sure of the exact site as indicated by the *temenu*, no error

of any kind being permitted. The texts were precise on this point: 'Not a finger more or less than the prescribed measurements.' It was usual to bury objects of different kinds along with the foundation text; in the case of his reconstruction of Etemenanki, Nabopolassar records that he deposited gold, silver, and precious stones.

Nabopolassar was a great builder king, and his sons had to prove to the Babylonians that they were worthy of their father. Thus they too turned to the task of reconstruction, joining with the workmen in carrying clay and mixtures of wine, oil and resin, and adjusting the head pad made of silver and gold.

There are some eloquent inscriptions on the foundation cylinders and elsewhere, by kings who restored the city and did not intend to be forgotten by an ungrateful posterity: 'Assurbanipal, the great king, the mighty king, king of the universe, king of Assyria, king of the four regions, king of kings, unrivalled prince, who, at the command of the gods, his allies, holds sway from the Upper to the Lower Sea, and has brought in submission at his feet all rulers . . . who made Babylon habitable again, rebuilt Esagila, renewed the sanctuaries of all the metropolises, who revived in them the ancient cults and restored their regular offerings which had ceased; grandson of Sennacherib, the great king, the mighty king, king of the universe, am I. . . . The unfinished work of Esagila, I finished. . . . Sometime, in the days to come, may the future prince, in the days of whose reign this work shall fall to ruins, restore its ruins. Let him inscribe my name alongside of his name. Let him look on my memorial, anoint it with oil, offer sacrifices and set it up beside his memorial. . . .'

There is the prayer of Neriglissar: 'Esagila and Ezida I beautified. The temples I placed in order. . . . The bronze serpents . . . on the doorways of Esagila which . . . are placed standing at the "Door of the Rising Sun", at the "Door of the Setting Sun", at the "Door of Abundance" . . . which no earlier king had erected, I the humble, the submissive, who am learned in the worship of the gods, have erected. Eight serpents . . . which hiss deadly poison against the nefarious and the foe, I have clothed with a covering of shining silver. . . . O Marduk, Lord, look with rejoicing upon my good works. . . . Grant me . . . a long life, fruitful posterity and the stability of my throne. . . .'

And before him, Nebuchadnezzar had written this moving prayer: 'Without thee, O my Lord, there is nothing. For the king whom thou lovest, whose name is on thy lips, who is pleasing to thee, thou hast prepared his name, keeping him in the way of righteousness. I am a prince who obeys thee, the creature of thy hand. Thou hast created me and hast entrusted to me the kingship over all peoples. May the fear of thy divine being be in my heart, and grant me that which it pleaseth thee, (for) thou art my creator.'

* * * * *

And so it has been with the whole story of civilization: the long struggle against total eclipse. But without death there can be no life. The pattern has never changed, there is one law that spans the history of man. Ambition, zeal, triumph, renown, defeat, and ruin, over and over again, make up the mighty epic of the eternal human struggle to survive. Not even the greatest civilization abiding for thousands of years has been able to prevail against the inscrutable will of the Almighty Creator of heaven and earth.

But the genius of the ancient races supplied the guiding principle of subsequent human behaviour. Their tyrannical gods, guardians of the people, are no more, their dynasties and empires have vanished, their civilization is dead. Yet, in the immense and poignant silence which abides, we should accord them that great honour which is their due. In the valley of the Tigris and Euphrates, the Eden of Semitic legend, the city of Babylon was built 'in the beginnings of time', and became the garden and granary of Western Asia. Her early history is for the most part still unknown; but she became the heart and soul of the ancient world, a leader in the administration of justice and social security, a place of pilgrimage. Her civilization is dead. The prophecies were fulfilled, and Babylon, a city of life and colour and beauty, has become 'a solitude arid as the desert'. When Xenophon led his army into Babylonia, he searched for the site of Babylon and found her temples and palaces buried in sand. 'There,' he wrote, 'was a great city.' Lucian, when he asked to be shown this famous city of Babylon, was told: 'You ask to see Babylon, the city long since destroyed, but, my friend, it is now impossible to locate her former site.'

Nothing is left of Babylon now, apart from the few relics which look so out of place in our museums, the bas-reliefs and strange enamelled beasts in clear fresh colouring, thousands of bricks blackened with fire, a few statues of gods and scribes, some amulets, seals, stelae and boundary stones, and the innumerable tablets from her astonishing libraries and archives, perhaps her greatest legacy. Nothing remains of Babylon the city, of her gods or people; only the earth which bears her, the rich earth of Mesopotamia. History is without pity. . . .

EPILOGUE

'By this River, the citie Bagdat is very aboundantly furnished with all kinds of provision, both with Corne, Flesh, Fowle, Fish, and Venison of all sorts; besides great store of Fruit, but especially of dates, and that cheape. This citie by some is called New Babylon, and may well be, because it did rise out of the ruines of old Babylon, not farre distant, being nothing so great nor so fair: for it contaynes in circuit but three English miles; and is built but of Bricke, dried in the Sunne; their houses also being flat-roofed and low.' (Account by John Cartwright, from *Purchas his Pilgrimes*, of a visit to Baghdad in A.D. 1603).

OVER two thousand years have elapsed since Babylon was left to the mercy of the elements. But history has shown that this is a region destined to be fertile, not only in 'all kinds of provision', but in the raising of cities famous in the annals of the world. After Seleucia, founded by the Macedonians and destroyed by the Romans, and Ctesiphon, founded by the Sassanians and destroyed by the Parthians, there is a gap of barely a hundred years before the founding of Baghdad under the Abbassid Caliphate.

Baghdad, whose very name seems fragrant as date wine, was the greatest capital of Islam. Its mediaeval splendour and rich intellectual achievement recall the greatest days of Babylon. Scholars, grammarians, astronomers, doctors and poets thronged the city, which for many centuries remained the great religious centre of the Oriental world. Like Babylon it was to suffer a series of invasions, the last of which, in the seventeenth century, completed the ruin of the city, whose palaces with their golden cupolas Harun al Rashid had once pointed out to one of his viziers, saying: 'From the East to the West I know of no happier city, nor a richer, than Baghdad.'

Baghdad today is once more a busy, prosperous city, its alleyways swarming with merchants, religious teachers, workmen and coppersmiths, and rich with the smell of frying kebabs, spices and sweetmeats. The storehouses and bazaars are piled high with the flea-haunted bales of Central Asia, dimly visible in the light of small smoking lamps which hardly serve to light these vaults that are full of unimagined treasures. In the open shop-fronts, pipes are smoked and anecdotes exchanged. These fascinating tales, mingling with the spicy scents of the bazaars, carry one back to the mediaeval past with its warriors and chivalrous combat, and its beautiful doe-eyed maidens that figure like sugar-plums in the accounts of mediaeval Baghdad.

Here is to be found the public letter-writer, who has set up his place next to the pipe-seller and is philosophically awaiting his customers. He does a brisk trade in letters of all kinds, but specializes in the finer literary variety, spiced with quotations from the classics, and his eloquence is only halted when the supply of money fails. Lightly the words will dance under his pen, like djinns pirouetting, and by these means the lovers will be bewitched. How many times already has he compared the betrothed of Jafar, of Saladin, or Ali the one-eyed, with a series of delicate things such as the velvety moon, or the roses of the gardens of Ispahan, whose petals are less fragile than the cheeks of the beloved? This public scribe, whose pockets are full of specimen copies (for the style, see tariff) will be, for the whole of his life, the lovers' instrument of fate. Honeyed words flow from him with ease, and he fulfils a very real need in a country where the cobbler on the corner and the blacksmith alike know by heart the odes of Hafiz or Saadi, but without the assistance of the scribe are unable to transmit their ideas on paper.

In the streets the Armenians carry water-skins filled with liquorice water, whose praises they sing in terms indistinguishable from those used by our friend the poet close at hand. In the markets there are sweetmeat stalls, their wares dripping with delicious Baghdad honey, with Turkish leather slippers and spiced sausages on sale close by. In front of the bakers' ovens a variety of wares are piled up, thin parchment-like sheets, circular flat cakes, and rounded loaves, waiting to be spread with onions, spices and olives. It is here that the Bedouins come to purchase their supplies, coming away with bread dipped in raisin syrup or sesame, or spread with tomato purée and sardines. The walls of the cafés leave a certain amount to be desired; the whole place reeks of aniseed. Here one can listen to the songs of Urfa, the city where the carp is sacred, sung to the tireless accompaniment of mandolins.

An unending hum of activity goes on outside. The sellers of sherbet, with their shining brass vessels, announce their presence by the musical clinking of their cups. In the saddlers' quarters the craftsmen crouch in dark corners stitching high saddles for camels and engraving on girths and bridles verses of the Koran, to remind the faithful that even in the desert they are in the hand of Allah. A group of apprentices not far away are joking together as they bend over their work; they are making nails. Everyone seems to be enjoying himself as he plies his traditional trade.

Baghdad, today the capital of Iraq, is still the eternal East, with its holy men, caravans, sweetmeat sellers, and oriental music, its dusty days and animated nights, its crowded alleyways tinged with the magic hues of dusk. Twilight transforms the river to an opalescent splendour as it glides swiftly by the ancient Caliphate city with an escort of *keleks* that follow it down from Mosul. And suddenly, without transition, it is night, sparkling everywhere with stars in the deep blue vault of the sky.

Mosul. . . . The Tigris separates it from the ancient site of Nineveh, built high upon the opposite bank. To the west of the river stretches the Jebel Sinjar region, haunt of the nomadic tribes. In the history of Mesopotamia the nomads have always played an important part, at times enjoying considerable political power. At one time a chief might have had as many as 37,000 tents under his rule, sheltering a nomadic population of about 200,000. He would have been able to rally a fighting force of something like 50,000 young enthusiasts only too ready to defend the prestige of their lord and kinsmen.

The nomads live constantly on the move, forever shifting their grazing grounds, often encroaching on land belonging to settled populations. Disputes over pasture and stock have been one of the major problems of administration in the country for thousands of years. When the bedouins set up camp the men sit around in a lordly fashion while the women do all the work. The little black tents, made from the hair of goat and camel, are quickly and deftly put up, and the women hurry away, surrounded by their brats, to fill their water-skins. Urine from the camels is used to bath the babies; they wash their hair in it too, as it is said to produce a fine lustre and to act as a disinfectant. Fires are soon lit all over the camp; when wood is not available the bedouin tribes use camel dung, which takes the form of large flat cakes rather like the sort of biscuit eaten on special feast days. This handy substitute for fuel gives off an acrid smoke. A fire is still regarded by itinerant tribes today as indicative of power and wealth, and the more fires there are in his camp the greater the esteem in which the chief—or sheikh—should be held by the notables of the district. The nomads set great store by the marks of good breeding, and the wandering chieftain is second to none in his observance of those finer details which betoken it, such as the long fringed carefully braided hair and the use of kohl as an eye cosmetic.

As soon as the fire is ready, a huge platter of *kous-kous*, which forms the main dish, is brought in by slaves, and they all squat round to devour the delicate morsels soaked in mutton fat. Nobody says a word; they are all much too intent on the matter in hand. Everyone digs into the rice, which has to be rolled into convenient pellets and then thrown with great speed into the mouth. A desert meal has none of the refinements of a banquet, and it is no place for the amateur. You simply wolf it down. But it is always necessary to appear well-bred, and if you want to make a good showing as a guest at one of these repasts you must never forget that it is respectable to belch at regular intervals. In some circles, of course, this would be frowned upon, but here it is regarded as an expression of appreciation and goodwill, in which all can share; everyone thus becomes pleasantly relaxed and cheerful, ready to enjoy an evening of light-hearted argument, or better still, to listen to the poet of the tribe recounting the great adventures of the past.

For the nomads poetry is indispensable; it accompanies all their activities. For the tribal poet, by some secret inimitable power, can transform the hot bare earth by the magic of words and disperse the dust and the wind, evoking close to the camp the green fresh image of an oasis in a sultry place. But woe to the evil-doers of the tribe! Hell, no less than heaven, can be evoked, dark, unending, a place of unmitigated torture. The great mysterious night may well be enlivened with tales of the damned, the shades, the djinns, waters that seethe, cauldrons packed with accursed ones, towering columns of flames, hungry monsters waiting to pounce, all the torments and sufferings that are to be the lot of the sinner in the world to come.

Poetry certainly seems to have its home in the East. Magic is abroad in the evening light; the imagination takes wings in response to the seductive luminous realm of the many-coloured dusk, the daily miracle of the Asian world. The mysterious basalt stelae of the Hittites matter nothing to the nomad, nor do the paintings found at Dura-Europos or the dancing figures of Assyrian angels from Til Barsib. For him the universe eternally consists in the motion of his steed and the pleasures of reverie; his soul is bared before the tremendous emptiness of the sky. He is well aware that the mountain and the sand and the oasis are all as changing as are the faces he sees around him, and that true power is vested only in the visionary. His father taught him the 200 words which make up his basic vocabulary, such as 'snake', 'lion', 'sword'. In his youth he learnt songs from distant lands, age-old songs declaimed by the tribes when Nineveh was in flames and the palace buildings crumbled over the national gods. His memory is infallible; he knows these poems of his ancestors by heart, line by line. It is thus that the genius of the races is transmitted over countless years by poems and songs and prophecies that exalt the heart. Damage and destruction may be the fate of royal inscriptions carved in stone; their message of victory and violence may be lost forever, carried off as the south wind chases the djinns. But through all tumult and upheaval the songs of the wandering peoples of Mesopotamia have survived the passing of time.

The desert lyrics may seem slightly tedious to us, because their themes are necessarily limited in range and tend to be repeated over and over again, rather like the arabesques whose rhythm is sometimes difficult for us to follow in the palaces of the Moorish kings. Western poetry tends to be rather more mystical and has a wider range of ideas. But we can still nevertheless appreciate the Arabic poetry of everyday life. Much of it is of a high standard, and in some cases of finer calibre than the somewhat abstruse variety favoured by the Western intelligentsia. It is also extremely popular. The Arab poet makes up his verses as he goes along, instead of withdrawing into a visionary seclusion. He does not set out to achieve a masterpiece; he makes up his poems for the sheer joy of doing so. His purpose is to enthral his listeners, to hold them spellbound. He can make his words dance in a magic circle. He is essentially the voice of his people, beloved by them and expressing their need to escape from reality, obeying an instinct peculiar to his race from earliest times. And it is thus that poetry spreads through the world, by a thousand hidden mysterious paths, becoming a necessity to man and at the same time lucrative.

Today on the banks of the Tigris and Euphrates, where so many forgotten capitals lie buried still, it is the same wherever you go. In the shadow of a Kurdish or Circassian tent, where you will be welcomed with a bowl of camel's milk; in the minute coffee-houses, where you can smoke the *narguileh* and watch the small swaying copper-coloured dancers; in the steppeland of Iraq, or in the north on the ancient highways of the Romans that skirt the Jaghjagha or the Habur rivers; on the former frontiers of Shalmaneser, Sennacherib, Septimus Severus, or Diocletian; in the shadow of the remains of Sargon's palace at Khorsabad; beside the sanctuary of

the Palmyran gods at Dura-Europos; by the mound of Susa; at
Resafa in the midst of the Syrian desert, the holy city; in the
Hauran, where the handsome Roman legionaries of long ago
spread the cult of Mithras with no less fervour than in the Rhine-
land or along the Danube; near Abu Kemal where the Sassanian
ruins abound, or in the forbidden solitudes of Yemen. . . . Everywhere, amongst rich and poor alike, you come across poets of
distinction and renown, whose mission it is to preserve the tribal
treasure-house of dreams.

There are those who despise the nomads, because they are not
eager to be assimilated into our civilization of nuclear explosives, or
perhaps because they decline to accept what amounts to a condition
of slavery, although it must not be openly recognized as such.
People are apt to look down on them for their camel-hair tents and
their simple way of life so alien to conventional society. These
wandering people have been on the move from the beginnings of
history; they have always been there, on their unfriendly land,
obeying today as in antiquity the laws of the seasonal cycle. This
perpetual restless movement of tribes towards the present frontiers
of the West is in these days peaceful enough; but many will
remember that these are the descendants of the nomadic tribes who
swept through Asia, the North African coast, and Spain. They were
the sword of Islam, its military genius and its untiring strength.
The days of their greatness are not forgotten by the nomads themselves; they remember Baghdad, where Greece sent her manu-
scripts and her philosophers; Damascus, 'The Great White Silent
One'; Cairo, 'The City of Victories'. Saladin who took Jerusalem
from the Christians; and Cordoba, Toledo and Granada, whose loss
is still lamented today in the *casbahs* of purple and gold and in the
bazaars of Marrakesh.

Mesopotamia has always been a place of legend; her poets who
sing of a prodigious past are richly endowed by tradition. Some of
their stories are based on lore as old as history itself, preserved and
adapted in the course of thousands of years of dramatic recitation
against the deep blue shadow of the camp. In the desert region
south of Mosul, where the nomads of old resented the power of the
city-states and empires, the Shammar troubadours of today have a
favourite tale: 'The father and chief of the Adites was called
Ad. He settled in the desert not long before the confusion of
tongues. There he founded a city. . . . His palaces were made of
gold, and he raised to heaven gardens that were more beautiful than
those of Babylon. Flowers and fruits were to be found there in

abundance. Birds, fashioned by the hand of man, perched in the branches of the trees. Their bodies, stuffed with sweet perfumes, made fragrant the air of the entire city. Ad was proud of that which he had done. He believed himself to be a god, and desired that others should worship him. But heaven did not permit this pride to go unpunished and he was struck by lightning. The city still exists in the desert, as an eternal sign of divine justice, but it is invisible to all eyes.'

The city still exists in the desert, but it is invisible to all eyes. . . . One cannot help wondering whether it is not towards this city of long ago that the nomads of today are constantly making their way, just as their ancestors did many thousands of years ago. The idea obviously fascinates them. Their endless journeying across monotonous tracts of arid land leaves plenty of time for meditation; poetry seems to be inborn in them, and life seems like a river which carries them along, smoothly and noiselessly, towards the floating cities which they have seen so many times vanish into the sky. They are like the people of the Bible; their ceaseless questing recalls the beginnings of human struggles. To see these people gathering together under one of their tents to listen to the poet of the tribe is an unforgettable experience: it is as though one had returned to the remote past.

INDEX